The
Ultimate Brownie
Book

Other books by
Bruce Weinstein

The Ultimate Candy Book

The Ultimate Ice Cream Book

The Ultimate Party Drink Book

Other books by
Bruce Weinstein and
Mark Scarbrough

The Ultimate Shrimp Book

The Ultimate Brownie Book

Bruce Weinstein & Thousands of Ways

Mark Scarbrough to Make America's

Favorite Treat, including Blondies,

Frostings, and Doctored Brownie Mixes

WILLIAM MORROW

An Imprint of HarperCollins*Publishers*

HarperCollins books may be purchased for educational, business, or sales promotional use. For information please write: Special Markets Department, HarperCollins Publishers Inc., 10 East 53rd Street, New York, NY 10022.

FIRST EDITION

Designed by Mary Austin Speaker

Printed on acid-free paper

Library of Congress Cataloging-in-Publication Data has been applied for.

ISBN 0-06-093761-0

02   03   04   05   06   QF   10   9   8   7   6   5   4   3   2   1

To Harriet Bell, for believing us and in us

Contents

Acknowledgments

Many, many thanks to

Debbie Weinstein, Esther Lou Scarbrough, and Ada McElhenney for trying out draft recipes and offering suggestions on how to better them.

David Sisson, Scott Stevens, Maya Kaimal, Laura Stanley, and Alethea Worden for eating their way through batch after batch.

Susan Ginsburg at Writers House for constant advice and encouragement.

Annie Leuenberger at Writers House for understanding that writers need their checks—now.

Karen Ferries for painstaking yet kind attention to the details, time and again.

Mary Austin Speaker and Roberto de Vicq de Cumptich at HarperCollins for once again designing an ultimate winner.

Ann Cahn and Karen Lumley at HarperCollins for producing our books with grace and style.

Carrie Weinberg, Gypsy Lovett, and James Haggerty at HarperCollins, publicists who keep the ultimate series alive and well.

Kate Stark at HarperCollins, for making sure the books keep flying out of the warehouse.

Katherine Ness, a kind, gracious, patient, and tireless copy editor.

Beatriz da Costa, a photographer with an unflinching eye.

David Weinstein, Lisa Aiello, Ned Wyss, Simma Park, and Clarissa Patrianova at Vox Design in New York, without a doubt the finest design firm in the city.

Brian Maynard at KitchenAid for the second mixer (one truly wasn't enough).

Karen Graves and Kay Emel-Powell at General Mills/Betty Crocker for cases and cases of mix—we lived with The Great Wall of box mixes for months and were never happier.

Robert Steinberg at Scharffen Berger Chocolate Makers for generously supplying some of the world's best chocolate, and for introducing us to nibs.

The doormen and concierges at London Terrace Apartments in Manhattan—proof positive that people never tire of eating brownies.

Nancy Vang, James Fox, Michael O'Neill, Eileen Shapiro, Eileen Macholl, Deb Reiner, Janet Zaleon, and the rest of the Stonewall Chorale in New York City—who knew so many pans of brownies could be eaten so quickly?

The
Ultimate Brownie
Book

Introduction

If brownies weren't real, we'd have to make them up. Both fudge and cake, they're part confection, part pastry. In other words, they're the stuff of dreams.

To warp William Blake's riff on the Tyger: "What immortal hand or eye dare concoct such awesome richness?" For us as for him, answers are few; so stories abound. Here's one: A Bangor, Maine, housewife was so excited by her latest creation that she forgot to put on her mitts, reached into the oven, and promptly dropped an extra-rich chocolate sheet cake right on the floor. Naturally, the cake collapsed. (She, too?) Undeterred, and with Yankee frugality, she served it anyway—and so began dropping all her cakes, although she never again forgot her oven mitts.

Or how about this one? Nineteenth-century midwestern farmwomen considered it a sin to waste food, although better farming methods were making for greater and greater production. Unfortunately, home refrigeration hadn't caught up with other technologies, so all that extra butter and eggs spoiled far too quickly. To solve the problem, these economical housewives began putting extra in their cookie batters, although they had to balance that richness with additional chocolate. The result? Dense little cakes, buttery and fudgy.

Or did you hear the one about the New York chef who accidentally dropped chocolate into a brown sugar cake? Or the French chef who had to make a dessert he thought would satisfy American fat-cat tycoons visiting Paris to promote President McKinley's trade policies?

Such are the myths. Here's what we know: Blondies actually came first, followed by brownies as a variation. Today we might think of blondies as brownies without a chocolate batter, as if blondies were just an afterthought, a simplification of the original. But Fannie Farmer, that American culinary pioneer, wrote the first known recipe in the 1896 *Boston Cooking-School Cook Book*. And what she proposed had no chocolate in it at all. Instead, molasses-rich cakes were browned in small individual tins. Thus the name: "brownies."

In 1897 the Sears, Roebuck catalog featured "brownies" by mail order only, but these cookies were nothing like what we call brownies, or even blondies for that matter. They weren't made from chocolate at all, but were instead named after J. Palmer Cox's cartoon characters, so popular in the Gilded Age. The cookies were probably variants of "melt-aways," an American classic that disappears in your mouth like those little elves in the forest.

Why no chocolate brownies? Believe it or not, chocolate was considered unhealthy, even sinful, in many nineteenth-century circles. It was associated with the French. (Horrors!) And it was railed against as a mind-altering drug. (We couldn't agree more.)

Fortunately the turn of the last century brought new ideas. Frankly, Americans were becoming more cosmopolitan. So by the 1906 edition of the Fanny Farmer cookbook, chocolate had been added to that original brownie recipe—but the name remained the same. And by 1916, Maria Parloa, one of the founders of the Boston Cooking School, had adapted some of Fannie Farmer's unpublished notes to write a chocolaty brownie recipe for a pamphlet to be distributed by Walter Baker & Company, the progenitor of Baker's Chocolate, then of Dorcester, Massachusetts.

There were yet more changes on the culinary horizon. As technology advanced and home ovens got larger, baking pans did too. So the brownie changed—no longer in little individual tins, but now a sheet cake. And as American affluence rose in this F. Scott Fitzgerald world, so did our taste for rich meals, rich desserts. Recipes for brownies indicate that the cakes were becoming so heavy with butter, they would collapse in on themselves. And so the fudgy brownie was born.

By the roaring 1920s, the brownie craze was full-blown. Recipes were splashed in newspaper columns, peppered in food-industry pamphlets, and elevated to culinary status at restaurants like "21" and Delmonico's in New York City. Since those days, the brownie's popularity has never lulled. It's been sparked by state fair bake-offs and celebrity endorsements. Liz Smith once ran Katherine Hepburn's brownie recipe in the *New York Post*, instigating a national craze long before the Internet made such things everyday.

Brownies and blondies may well be the quintessential American treats: perfect for family gatherings, parties, and picnics. These dense cakes freeze well, travel easily in a get-up-and-go society, and taste like heaven, despite being quick and easy every time.

HOW TO USE THIS BOOK

As in the other Ultimate books in this series, the recipes here are alphabetical—but with a slight difference. Rather than one booklong list, there are four chapters of recipes: brownies, blondies, easy icings, and fun with brownie mixes.

Within each chapter the recipes are still alphabetical. And they are all basics—nothing frou-frou or esoteric. The point is to make old-fashioned, straightforward treats: chocolate syrup brownies, cream cheese blondies, seven minute frosting. (Of course, we hope some of the basics surprise you: chile brownies, fruitcake blondies, cola icing.)

Each of these basics then becomes the platform for variations. Here's where the real fun begins. So many things that can be added to a brownie batter! As we worked on the book, we ended up with long lists of variations: Walnut Applesauce Brownies, Cranberry Applesauce Brownies, Cranberry Walnut Applesauce Brownies, Ginger Cranberry Walnut Applesauce Brownies, and on and on and on. So we've shifted the format a bit. After each recipe, there's a list of possible additions (spices, flavorings, and mix-ins) in the amount appropriate for the given pan size and batter volume. You can choose among them at will. With so many possibilities, there's surely a lifetime of brownie recipes here.

We hope you have as much fun baking these treats as we did testing the recipes. You cannot imagine the hundreds of trays that came out of a small Manhattan kitchen for months on end! No matter how many we brought to friends' homes and offices, people never seemed to tire of brownies. They even seemed miffed if we thought we shouldn't impose with one more tray. Hundreds of pounds of butter and chocolate later, we know from personal experience the lasting appeal of these American favorites.

Special Equipment, Ingredients, and Tips for Success

SPECIAL EQUIPMENT

BAKING PANS. Almost every recipe in this book calls for one of three pan sizes: an 8-inch square, a 9-inch square, and a 9 × 13-inch rectangle. Always use the pan size called for—make no substitutions here. The recipes, of course, have been developed with a specific pan size in mind: smaller ones for more esoteric brownies, larger ones for crowd-pleasers. We prefer standard commercial-grade aluminum baking pans—even over nonstick pans, which can scratch easily (once that happens, they conduct heat unevenly and, worse yet, may pose health problems). As for glass pans, they tend to overbake the edges of brownies, superheating the chocolate there in suspension, causing it to burn and turn bitter. If you do use glass, reduce the oven temperature by 25 degrees to avoid this problem. The baking time, however, will most likely not change, since glass heats so efficiently.

CHOCOLATE CHOPPER. This handy metal tool looks like a mini pitchfork, with three to five prongs that are not sharp but are heavy enough to break up a five-pound bar of chocolate. For this task, a chocolate chopper is far superior to a knife: (1) It conserves chocolate, making less dust; and (2) it doesn't bend or dull, as a knife might.

KITCHEN SCALE. This invaluable tool will allow you to have the exact amount of chocolate needed for a recipe, whether you're using blocks, morsels, or chips. Make sure it's set to ounces, not grams.

MIXERS. Many of the recipes in this book offer you a choice for mixing batters: either by hand with a wooden spoon, or with an electric mixer. Particularly if you have arthritis or a connective tissue disorder, a mixer is invaluable for creating a smooth batter. If you have no such problems, here's a rule of thumb: Hand-mixing makes denser, fudgier brownies; machine mixing makes lighter, more tender brownies. If you choose the latter, we recommend a stand mixer, rather than a handheld portable. Use one with at least a 4½-quart bowl.

CAKE TESTER. You can use either a metal cake tester, sold in gourmet markets and specialty cooking stores, or a wooden toothpick. If you use a metal cake tester, be sure it's clean and dry each time. If you use a toothpick, never reuse it—get a fresh one each time.

OFFSET SPATULA. Made of metal or heat-safe rubber, this is a long thin spatula with a crook in the blade about two inches from the handle. By slipping an offset spatula under brownies or blondies, you can remove them from the pan with little crumbling.

SPECIAL INGREDIENTS

BANANA CHIPS. These are fried or dried banana chips, sometimes sweetened, sometimes not. The sweetened variety is available in most supermarkets near the dried fruit; the unsweetened, in gourmet and health-food stores. In this book you may use either, depending on your taste—but don't confuse them with plantain chips, which are salty, like potato chips.

BUTTER. The recipes call for unsalted butter, the baking standard. Because of either dietary or religious concerns, you may substitute equivalent amounts of margarine, although your final product will be heavier and denser.

Also, you may use some solid vegetable shortening. This is an old trick of professional bakers, who want a firmer cake to hold up under loads of frosting; hydrogenated shortening will increase the dough's elasticity, making a sturdier brownie. Use half the butter called for, and replace the other half with an equivalent amount of solid vegetable shortening, such as Crisco.

CANDY BARS. Many recipes are varied by adding chopped candy bars. Use a heavy chef's knife to chop them into ½-inch pieces for better incorporation and melting.

CHILE POWDER. One recipe in this book, and many variations, calls for pure chile powder, the kind made only from ground chiles. Conventional chile powder, sold in most supermarkets, contains oregano and cumin, as well as ground chiles. Pure chile powder is found in gourmet markets and in Latin American and Mexican markets.

You can also make your own. Buy ancho chiles (that is, dried poblano chiles), remove the stems, cut the chiles open, and scoop out the seeds. Grind the shells in a food grinder, with a mortar and pestle, or in a coffee grinder. Store the pure chile powder in a tightly covered jar in a dark, cool place for up to three months. (To remove the taste and odor from the grinder, after emptying the pure chile powder, fill the grinder with rice. Process to a fine dust and wipe clean.)

CHOCOLATE. This book is unabashedly written by chocolate lovers for chocolate lovers. Frankly, the recipes are heavy-handed with chocolate. The brownies are stuffed with it; all the blondie recipes call for chocolate chips.

Long ago, we were slaves to other brownie recipes that called for two, maybe three, ounces of chocolate for a 9 × 13-inch pan. "What's the point?" we asked ourselves. Sure, for a cake lover, those barely brown brownies might fit the bill. But for a chocolate lover? No way. We want chocolate, and lots of it.

We call for six kinds of chocolate: **bittersweet, semisweet, Mexican, milk, unsweetened,** and **white**. We recommend you use the finest chocolate you can comfortably afford. After all, the better the chocolate, the better the brownie. In any case, use unadulterated chocolate, not cut with hydrogenated oils; read the label before buying.

Many recipes ask you to select either **bittersweet** or **semisweet chocolate,** depending on your taste. Admittedly, it's a complicated choice. First off, there are no governmental standards to differentiate between bittersweet and semisweet—what one manufacturer labels "bitter," another might label "semisweet." It all has to do with the percentage of cocoa solids and cocoa butter in the final mixture—but it's by no means clear where the lines of labeling lie. Fortunately, premium brands of chocolate give the amount of combined cocoa solids and cocoa butter as a percentage on the label. We believe 70% is excellent bittersweet; 62%, excellent semisweet. One question we're often asked: If semisweet chocolate is labeled 62%, what's the remaining 38%? It's mostly the sugar and vanilla extract, added to flavor and bind the chocolate.

In the end, although we give you the choice in every recipe, we prefer melted bittersweet chocolate in brownies and semisweet chocolate chips in blondies. In brownies, the additional tang of the bittersweet balances the butter and eggs, helping the treats taste deeper, richer, and less cloyingly sweet. In blondies, the semisweet chips give them their classic sweetness.

Two varieties of either 62% semisweet or 70% bittersweet chocolate can taste remarkably different. First off, there's a wide variety of formulas for chocolate making (the exact amount of additional cocoa butter in the bar is each chocolate maker's closely guarded secret). There are also manufacturing differences, including the weight of the grinder, the variety of the cocoa beans, their country of origin, the grinding time, the roasting time, and the amount of added soy lecithin (a stabilizer sometimes used). The best advice is to do some taste-testing on your own.

So-called **Mexican chocolate,** often sold under the brand name Ibarra, is a flavorful combination of dark chocolate, cinnamon, and cocoa nibs (see below). Available in gourmet stores and Latin American markets, it is used in only one base recipe here, but in several variations.

Milk chocolate, obviously enough, adds whole milk to the chocolate mixture—which unfortunately gives milk chocolate a shorter shelf-life than, say, semisweet chocolate. Always smell and taste a small bit of the milk chocolate before proceeding with a recipe—if it has a sharp whang, like soured milk, it's beyond its prime.

But when it's fresh, milk chocolate makes an extraordinarily rich brownie; and milk chocolate chips are an extravagant mix-in for any recipe.

Unsweetened chocolate is often labeled "99% cocoa solids." The remaining 1% is the small amount of vanilla and stabilizers added to the chocolate mixture. Although you might think the taste of unsweetened chocolate is uniform across the industry (after all, "un" is "un," right?), there's actually a wide range of tastes, depending on the cocoa bean used. Some beans have more oil, some less; some are starchier, some astringent. Even how the beans are roasted affects the final taste. And the amount of cocoa butter added will greatly affect the "finish" (that is, the aftertaste, the way the chocolate coats your tongue). What's more, unsweetened chocolate can also be flavored with nuts, vanilla, or even coffee—for these recipes, always buy unflavored unsweetened chocolate.

White chocolate contains cocoa butter without any other cocoa solids. Purists refuse out of hand to acknowledge that it's even chocolate. We guard no such bogeymen, but offer only this advice: Buy white chocolate made with cocoa butter, not cut with hydrogenated oil.

CHOCOLATE CHIPS. These days, chocolate chips are available in many sizes and flavors. Basically, regular or mini chips will work in any of these recipes; chocolate chunk chips are fine for melting but are too large for mixing in. Flavored chips, including mint and raspberry, make good mix-ins but should not be melted for the base batter. White chocolate chips are often cut with hydrogenated fat. If a better variety is not available in your market, buy premium white chocolate bars and chop them into small pieces for mix-ins.

COCOA NIBS. A relatively new product in the U.S., cocoa nibs are coarsely ground cocoa beans. The very germ of chocolate, cocoa nibs are nutty, slightly bitter, but still sweet. They will not melt, so they add a delicate crunch as a mix-in to a baked brownie or blondie. You can find cocoa nibs in most gourmet supermarkets and specialty baking stores.

FLOUR. Use only all-purpose flour for these recipes. We prefer unbleached. Neither cake flour nor self-rising flour is used in this book. If you store flour in the refrigerator, it should be returned to room temperature before proceeding with a recipe. Cold flour can shock melted chocolate, causing it to seize.

EXTRACTS AND FLAVORINGS. Many of these variations call for extracts, a staple in candy-making and professional baking but perhaps unfamiliar to the home cook. Generic brands, available in most supermarkets, can have an alcoholic aftertaste that doesn't always disappear in baking. Premium brands, such as those sold by Boyajian, offer a brighter taste and smoother finish (see Source Guide). Boyajian offers three mint extracts (peppermint, wintergreen, and spearmint)—you can thus alter your mint brownies based on your own taste. Boyajian does not offer banana, maple, or rum extracts. For these, try McCormick's line.

Almost every recipe calls for vanilla extract.

We recommend pure vanilla extract, not an imitation flavoring. Penzeys Spices makes a double-strength vanilla, perfect for those of us who routinely double the amount of vanilla in any recipe (see Source Guide).

NUTS AND NUT OILS. Use only fresh nuts in baking. The oven heat releases their oils into the batter. If the nuts are rancid, the batter will be too. And use only unsalted nuts, unless the salted variety is specifically called for. Unsalted nuts are available in many gourmet markets and most health-food stores.

As for nut oils, store them in the refrigerator. They may cloud, but they'll stay fresh longer. Always return them to room temperature before proceeding with a recipe.

PEPITÁS. These are green peeled pumpkin seeds, popular in Mexican sauces. When toasted gently in a skillet, they pop open and release a slightly sweet, buttery flavor. Baked, they soften somewhat, adding more aroma than crunch to the final brownie or blondie. Pepitás are available in Latin American, health-food, and most specialty stores in the nut section.

TOASTED CHICKPEAS. These healthy yet still crunchy treats are available in most East Indian markets; look for the unflavored, unsalted variety, as some are coated with curry powder or other spices. Toasted chickpeas add a starchy crunch to brownies, far different from the crackly crunch of nuts.

UNSWEETENED COCOA POWDER. To make cocoa powder, at least four-fifths of the cocoa butter is removed from ground cocoa paste. Some cocoa powders are "Dutch processed"—an alkali has been added to make the remaining cocoa solids both less bitter and more dissolvable. "Non-alkalized" cocoa powder is therefore more astringent and somewhat purer. You may use either for these recipes—but never use a cocoa powder that has sugar added.

TIPS FOR SUCCESSFUL BROWNIES

ALWAYS GREASE AND FLOUR THE PAN. You'll need to prepare the baking pan before you use it. Greasing and flouring the pan—even a nonstick one—will allow even baking because a barrier of fat has been placed between the batter and the hot pan. It also, of course, aids in easy removal once the treats are done.

You may use an aerosol spray with flour suspended in the oil, such as Baker's Joy, a brand available in most gourmet markets, baking supply stores, and specialty food shops. You may also do it the old-fashioned way. Here are some simple techniques:

To butter a pan: Place a small pat of butter on a piece of wax paper and rub it around the inside of the pan, completely covering the bottom, the sides, and the interior corners. Or use the butter wrapper when you've removed the stick; there's often enough left in two wrappers to grease a 9 × 13-inch pan.

To oil a pan: Place a dab of canola, corn, or vegetable oil on a paper towel and rub it around the inside of the pan, making sure you coat the corners. Vegetable oil sprays such as Pam can also be used. Just avoid the flavored variety.

To flour a pan: After buttering or oiling it, place 1 tablespoon flour in the pan and rotate the pan end to end, tapping it all the while, until the bottom and sides are thoroughly coated. Tilt the pan onto one side, gently rap the bottom to collect the extra flour in a corner, then discard that excess.

MIX THE DRY INGREDIENTS FIRST. Almost every recipe asks you to mix the dry ingredients in a separate bowl before you add them to the eggs, butter, or oil. Although this step dirties a second bowl, it ensures that the leavening is evenly distributed through the batter.

Adding already combined dry ingredients all at once also contributes to the cake's tenderness. The wet flour doesn't have a chance to become glutinous and thick while you search for the baking powder or salt. And the leavening agent can't get wet and start working inefficiently (without glutens present) while you're still measuring out the flour.

WEIGH THE CHOCOLATE. The amount of chocolate is given by weight, always in ounces. You can, of course, use the chocolate sold in grocery stores in 1-ounce squares; you then need only count out the number of squares to equal the quantity of ounces called for. You can also use chocolate morsels or chips—but you'll need to weigh them to be sure you have the right amount. On average, 3 ounces of chocolate chips equals about ½ cup, but there's a wide variety of shapes and sizes, from miniature chips to chunks. When chocolate chips are to be folded into a batter, rather than melted, we give both a weight and a volume amount (½

cup, 1 cup) in the ingredient list—in these cases, precision is not as crucial as when one melts chocolate for a batter.

MELT CHOCOLATE SLOWLY. The recipes give instructions on using a double boiler, or improvising if you don't have one. Chocolate should never be melted in a pan directly over a flame. Once scorched, chocolate turns rough and bitter.

As it melts, chocolate can unexpectedly resolidify into a hard lump. In culinary terms, it can "seize." If a small amount of steam escapes from the simmering water in a double boiler and then condenses into the melting chocolate, the chocolate crystals will instantly realign and adhere, turning the whole thing into a rock in the pan. If this happens, add cream or milk, 1 tablespoon at a time, stirring constantly in the double boiler still set over boiling water. Continue stirring until the hardened ball softens and remelts. The resulting mixture, while grainy, will work in the recipe. But do not use more than 4 tablespoons of liquid.

Very rarely, melted chocolate will seize when it's combined with other wet ingredients— usually because the eggs or other liquids were not at room temperature. If the chocolate seizes at this point, continue beating with a mixer at medium speed until the mixture is again smooth. To be honest, you'll need to hope for the best; if it doesn't smooth out, you'll have to start over.

YOU CAN MELT CHOCOLATE (AND BUTTER) IN A MICROWAVE. Place the chopped chocolate or chocolate chips and the butter, if using, in a large microwave-safe bowl. Microwave on High for 2 minutes, then stir the mixture with a rubber spatula, scraping down the sides of the bowl. Microwave on High for another minute, then check to see if half the chocolate is melted. If not, stir again and microwave on High for another minute. Once half the chocolate is melted, remove the bowl from the microwave and continue stirring until the chocolate (and butter) has completely melted.

SIFT UNSWEETENED COCOA POWDER. A fussy step, yes; but cocoa powder can clump—sometimes because of humidity, sometimes because of the alkali used in its processing. Sift the cocoa powder and you'll have no knots in your batter. Use either a traditional flour sifter or a fine-mesh sieve. In either case, sift the cocoa powder onto a large sheet of wax paper, then set it aside. When you're ready to use it, funnel it into the batter by curving the sheet into a "V." By not using an extra bowl, you'll save on cleanup afterwards.

TOAST NUTS BEFORE YOU ADD THEM TO A BATTER. Some suggested mix-ins call for toasted nuts ("chopped toasted hazelnuts," for example), which have a stronger, more piquant taste than raw nuts—which are, obviously, subtler, sometimes even softer, in a baked cake. *To toast nuts,* place them on a lipped cookie sheet in a preheated 350°F oven for 3 to 7 minutes. Toss them and continue baking until they begin to brown and give off a nutty, characteristic aroma, between 2 and 4 more minutes, tossing them once or twice to avoid scorching.

SPOON THE BATTER EVENLY INTO THE PAN. Don't just dump batter into the center of a prepared pan. If you do, you'll end up having to push it to the corners, thereby losing much of the aeration you've beaten into the batter. As you pour or spoon the batter out, move the bowl over the whole pan. If you still need to spread it, do so gently, with a rubber spatula or the back of a wooden spoon. Never press down into the batter.

WATCH THE BAKING TIMES, BUT DON'T TREAT THEM AS GIVEN LAW. Always check for doneness with a toothpick or cake tester, rather than simply relying on the timer's ding. Also, your oven may have a slight tilt. If so, gently rotate the baking pan halfway through the cooking process. Be careful not to shake it, or the brownies will fall.

BELIEVE IT OR NOT, YOU MAY WANT THEM TO FALL. Several recipes ask you to rap the pan against the oven rack halfway through baking so that the brownies collapse and become dense. Actually, you can do that with any recipe. Two-thirds of the way through the baking process, pick the baking pan up from both sides with oven mitts, rap it gently but firmly three or four times against the oven rack, and then finish out the prescribed baking time. The result will be a denser brownie, not necessarily fudgier (that's a matter of proportions among the chocolate, butter, and eggs) but more toothsome. Unfortunately, this trick does not work well with blondies. The resulting cake is simply too tough.

WHEN TESTING FOR DONENESS, AVOID THE MIX-INS. There may be chocolate chips or other wet ingredients in the batter. If so, it's best to test the cake in several places to make sure the cake is done. Always err on the side of underdone, rather than overdone. Brownies and blondies will set up as they cool—the center can be slightly wet, yet the final cake still quite fudgy and rich.

DON'T USE A METAL KNIFE ON NON-STICK COOKWARE. These recipes ask you to cut the brownies while they are still in the pan. If you're using nonstick cookware, you must be very careful not to scratch the finish. Use a plastic or rubber knife, specifically designed for this cookware and available in specialty markets and many supermarkets; or let the brownies cool completely and cut them with a stiff rubber spatula. In any event, do not press down into the nonstick surface—and be careful when removing them from the pan with a spatula.

If you're still worried about the pan's surface, remove the entire cake in one piece. To do so, let it cool completely, place a rack over the top of the pan, and turn the pan and rack over together. Knock the bottom of the pan once or twice with your hand, then gently lift the pan up. Place a second rack on top of the brownie cake, invert again, and remove the rack that used to be on the bottom. Then cut, store at room temperature, or freeze the brownies or blondies as desired. Brownies don't do well in the refrigerator—the glutens toughen, the butter coagulates, the cake is prone to picking up moisture and odors.

COOL THE BROWNIES COMPLETELY. Although they are wonderful warm, brownies—especially the fudgy ones—cut raggedly unless they're cooled. Some of the really fudgy versions offered here need to stand for up to two hours so the chocolate can set. For very fudgy results, you can even leave these in the pan overnight—if you have that much willpower.

TO ICE OR NOT TO ICE—THAT'S THE REAL QUESTION. And it's a matter of taste. We often give icing suggestions in the headnotes, but you can pick and choose at will—or forgo any icing at all. We don't, however, recommend freezing iced brownies; as they thaw, the icing turns the brownies boggy. All the icing or frosting recipes make enough for a 9 × 13-inch pan of brownies or blondies. If you make a smaller pan, you can either pile the icing on deeper, or you can use the leftover icing for cookies, graham crackers, or purchased cakes. In any event, brownies and blondies, like all cakes, must be completely cooled before they can be iced.

Brownies

Applesauce Brownies

Makes sixteen 2 × 2-inch brownies

Of all things, we start with a healthy brownie, one that's almost fat-free. (Don't worry—decadent treats are coming.) These are actually a hybrid: part quick bread, part brownie. Leavened with beaten egg whites, they're also guilt-free: no butter, no egg yolks, but still cakey, chewy, even a little sticky. Ice them with a light frosting, such as Brown Sugar Icing (page 148) or Seven Minute Frosting (page 164).

Vegetable oil for the pan
1½ cups sugar
1 cup all-purpose flour
¾ cup unsweetened cocoa powder, sifted
1 teaspoon baking powder
½ teaspoon baking soda
½ teaspoon salt
4 large egg whites, at room temperature
¾ cup plain applesauce
2 teaspoons vanilla extract

1. Position the rack in the middle third of the oven. Preheat the oven to 350°F. Oil an 8-inch square baking pan; set it aside.

2. In a large bowl, whisk the sugar, flour, cocoa powder, baking powder, baking soda, and salt until well combined. Set aside.

3. In a second large bowl, whisk the egg whites until foamy, about 1 minute; stir in the applesauce and vanilla until uniform and smooth. With a wooden spoon or a rubber spatula, stir the applesauce mixture into the flour mixture just until combined. Do not beat. Pour the batter into the prepared pan, spreading it gently to the corners.

4. Bake for 28 minutes, or until a toothpick or cake tester comes out with a few moist crumbs attached. Set the pan on a wire rack to cool for at least 30 minutes.

5. Cut the brownies into 16 squares while they're still in the pan. Carefully remove them

with an offset spatula. Serve immediately, or let cool completely before covering with plastic wrap for storage at room temperature. They will stay fresh for up to 4 days. The brownies can also be tightly wrapped in wax paper, sealed in a freezer-safe bag, and frozen for up to 3 months; allow them to thaw at room temperature before serving.

To vary this recipe
Whisk one or more of the following spices into the flour mixture:

1 tablespoon poppy seeds • 1 teaspoon ground cinnamon • ½ teaspoon ground cloves • ½ teaspoon ground ginger

and/or
Add one of the following flavorings with the vanilla:

1 tablespoon bourbon • 1 teaspoon grated lemon zest • ½ teaspoon maple extract • ½ teaspoon rum extract • ¼ teaspoon almond extract

and/or
Stir in ½ cup of any of the following mix-ins, or ½ cup any combination of the following mix-ins, with the flour mixture:

chopped dried apples • chopped pecans • chopped walnuts • crumbled gingersnap cookies • dried cherries • dried cranberries • granola • raisins • semisweet chocolate chips • slivered almonds • unsalted shelled sunflower seeds.

Banana Brownies

Makes twenty-four $2\frac{1}{4} \times 2\frac{1}{8}$-inch brownies

Ripe bananas and loads of chocolate make these brownies moist and dense, but you can make them even fudgier by forcing them to fall during baking. After 20 minutes' baking time, rap the pan against the oven rack three or four times; then allow to bake for the remaining 15 minutes undisturbed. Ice them with Chocolate Fudge Frosting (page 152) or Buttercream (page 150). Or for an adult version of a lunchbox favorite, frost them with Peanut Butter Icing (page 163).

¾ cup all-purpose flour, plus additional for the pan

½ teaspoon baking soda

½ teaspoon salt

8 tablespoons (1 stick) unsalted butter, plus additional for the pan, at room temperature

6 ounces bittersweet or semisweet chocolate, chopped, or semisweet chocolate chips

2 ounces unsweetened chocolate, chopped

¾ cup granulated sugar

½ cup packed light brown sugar

2 large eggs, at room temperature

1 teaspoon vanilla extract

2 ripe bananas, peeled and mashed (about 1 cup)

1 tablespoon banana liqueur (optional)

1. Position the rack in the lower third of the oven. Preheat the oven to 350°F. Butter and flour a 9 × 13-inch baking pan; set it aside.

2. In a medium bowl, whisk the flour, baking soda, and salt until well combined. Set aside.

3. Place 3 tablespoons butter and both kinds of chocolate in the top of a double boiler set over simmering water. If you don't have a double boiler, place 3 tablespoons butter and both kinds of chocolate in a heat-safe bowl that fits snugly over a small pot of simmering water. Stir constantly until half the butter and chocolate is melted. Remove the top of the double boiler or the bowl from the pot; then continue stirring, away from the heat, until the butter and chocolate are completely melted. Allow to cool for 10 minutes. (To melt chocolate in a microwave, see pages 9-10.)

4. Meanwhile, cream the remaining 5 tablespoons butter, granulated sugar, and brown sugar in a large bowl with an electric mixer at medium speed. Continue beating until the sugar has dissolved and the mixture is smooth, about 4 minutes, scraping down the sides of the bowl as necessary. Beat in the eggs one at a time, allowing the first to be thoroughly incorporated before adding the second. After beating in the second egg for 1 minute, add the vanilla, bananas, banana liqueur, if desired, and the chocolate mixture. Continue beating until the batter is smooth, about 2 minutes.

5. With a wooden spoon or rubber spatula, stir in the flour mixture just until combined. Do not beat. Spoon the batter into the prepared pan, spreading it gently to the corners.

6. Bake for 35 minutes, or until a toothpick or cake tester comes out with a few moist crumbs attached. Set the pan on a wire rack to cool for at least 30 minutes.

7. Cut the brownies into 24 pieces while they are still in the pan. Carefully remove them with an offset spatula. Serve immediately, or let cool completely before covering with plastic wrap for storage at room temperature. They will stay fresh for up to 4 days. The brownies can be tightly wrapped in wax paper, sealed in a freezer-safe bag, and frozen for up to 2 months; allow them to thaw at room temperature before serving.

To vary this recipe

Whisk 2 teaspoons ground cinnamon • or 1½ teaspoons pure chile powder into the flour mixture *and/or*

Substitute one of the following flavorings for the vanilla:

1 teaspoon coconut extract or flavoring • 1 teaspoon maple extract • 1 teaspoon rum extract *and/or*

Stir in 1¼ cups of any of the following mix-ins, or 1¼ cups any combination of the following mix-ins, with the flour mixture:

chopped caramels • chopped dried apricots • chopped dried figs • chopped dried prunes • chopped honey-roasted pecans • chopped roasted unsalted peanuts • chopped walnuts • cocoa nibs • peanut M & M's • Raisinets • semisweet chocolate chips • shredded sweetened coconut • toasted pepitás • white chocolate chips.

Black and White Brownies

Makes twenty-four $2\frac{1}{4} \times 2\frac{1}{8}$-inch brownies

For these checkerboard brownies, you actually make two batters: a dark chocolate one and a white chocolate. Depending on the day's humidity and the flour's glutens, the thin batters may run a bit, making their edges rougher, more like cobblestones in the pan. If you like to color outside the lines, you can make the edges even less defined by zigzagging a knife through them in the pan, making streaks of light and dark throughout. Because Black and White Brownies are so rich and buttery, they're best on their own, without an icing.

½ pound (2 sticks) unsalted butter, plus additional for the pan, at room temperature

7 ounces bittersweet or semisweet chocolate, chopped, or semisweet chocolate chips

7 ounces white chocolate, chopped, or white chocolate chips

2 cups sugar

2 teaspoons vanilla extract

4 large eggs, at room temperature

2 large egg yolks, at room temperature

2 cups all-purpose flour, plus additional for the pan

1 teaspoon baking powder

1 teaspoon salt

1. Position the oven rack in the lower third of the oven. Preheat the oven to 350°F. Butter and flour a 9 × 13-inch baking pan; set it aside.

2. Place 8 tablespoons (1 stick) butter and the dark chocolate in the top of a double boiler set over simmering water. If you don't have a double boiler, place 8 tablespoons butter and the dark chocolate in a heat-safe bowl that fits snugly over a small pot of simmering water. Stir constantly until half the butter and chocolate is melted. Remove the top of the double boiler or the bowl from the pot; then continue stirring, away from the heat, until the butter and chocolate are completely melted. Transfer the mixture to a large bowl to cool it. Wash the top of the double boiler or the heat-safe bowl. (To melt butter and chocolate in a microwave, see pages 9-10.)

3. Place the remaining 8 tablespoons (1 stick) butter and the white chocolate in the top of the double boiler, again set over simmering water, or in the heat-safe bowl, again set snugly over a pot of simmering water. Stir constantly until half the butter and white chocolate is melted. Remove the top of the double boiler or the bowl from the pot; then continue stirring, away from the heat, until the butter and white chocolate are completely melted. Transfer the mixture to a second large bowl and allow to cool slightly, about 5 minutes.

4. With a wooden spoon or a rubber spatula, stir 1 cup sugar, 1 teaspoon vanilla, 2 eggs, and

1 egg yolk into the cooled dark chocolate mixture. Continue stirring until well combined. Then stir in 1 cup flour, ½ teaspoon baking powder, and ½ teaspoon salt just until incorporated. The batter will be loose but sticky; set aside.

5. With a clean wooden spoon or rubber spatula, stir the remaining 1 cup sugar, 1 teaspoon vanilla, 2 eggs, and 1 egg yolk into the white chocolate mixture. Continue stirring until well combined. Then stir in the remaining 1 cup flour, ½ teaspoon baking powder, and ½ teaspoon salt just until incorporated.

6. To make the black and white brownies, spoon a checkerboard pattern of alternating dark and white batters into the prepared pan, in ⅔-cup amounts. You should end up with a 4 × 3 grid. The batter will run, creating uneven edges. Any remaining dark or white batter can be added to squares of its own color.

7. Bake for 35 minutes, or until a toothpick or cake tester comes out with many moist crumbs attached. The brownies may be soft at the center; they will set up as they cool. Set the pan on a wire rack to cool for at least 1 hour.

8. Cut the brownies into 24 pieces while they're still in the pan. Carefully remove them with an offset spatula. Serve immediately, or let cool completely before covering with plastic wrap for storage at room temperature. They will stay fresh for up to 3 days. The brownies can be tightly wrapped in wax paper, sealed in a freezer-safe bag, and frozen for up to 3 months; allow them to thaw at room temperature before serving.

To vary this recipe
Stir one or more of the following herbs and spices into each of the batters with the flour:
1 teaspoon finely chopped fresh mint leaves • 1 teaspoon chopped fresh sage • ½ teaspoon ground cinnamon
and/or
Stir ½ cup of any of the following mix-ins, or ½ cup any combination of the following mix-ins, into each of the batters with the flour mixture: butterscotch chips • chopped Butterfinger bars • chopped candied chestnuts • chopped hazelnuts • chopped Heath bars • cocoa nibs • crumbled Oreo cookies • mint chocolate chips • peanut butter chips • Reese's Pieces • semisweet chocolate chips • yellow raisins.

Bourbon Brownies

Makes twenty-four $2\frac{1}{4} \times 2\frac{1}{8}$-inch brownies

Although bourbon truffles are a holiday tradition among great aunts and grandmothers, these brownies—with that classic combination of dark chocolate and bourbon—are perfect any time of year. They're rich but surprisingly delicate, a little cakey, with good crumb. For a deep flavor, use a premium bourbon like Maker's Mark or Jack Daniel's Black Label.

1 cup all-purpose flour, plus additional for the pan
½ teaspoon baking powder
½ teaspoon salt
12 ounces bittersweet or semisweet chocolate, chopped, or semisweet chocolate chips
½ pound (2 sticks) unsalted butter, plus additional for the pan, at room temperature
1 cup packed light brown sugar
2 large eggs, at room temperature
½ cup bourbon

1. Position the rack in the lower third of the oven. Preheat the oven to 350°F. Butter and flour a 9×13-inch baking pan; set it aside.

2. In a medium bowl, whisk the flour, baking powder, and salt. Set aside.

3. Place the chocolate in the top of a double boiler set over simmering water. If you don't have a double boiler, place the chocolate in a heat-safe bowl that fits snugly over a small pot of simmering water. Stir constantly until half the chocolate is melted. Remove the top of the double boiler or the bowl from the pot; then continue stirring, away from the heat, until the chocolate is completely melted. Allow to cool for 5 minutes. (To melt chocolate in the microwave, see pages 9–10.)

4. In a large bowl, cream the butter and brown sugar with a wooden spoon or with an electric mixer at medium speed. Beat until smooth and light, about 9 minutes by hand or 5 minutes with a mixer. Beat in the eggs one at a time, allowing the first to be thoroughly incorporated before adding the second. Beat for 1 minute, then add the bourbon and melted chocolate, beating until the batter is smooth and pale.

5. With a wooden spoon or a rubber spatula, stir in the flour mixture just until incorporated. Do not beat. Spoon the batter into the prepared pan, spreading it gently to the corners.

6. Bake for 25 minutes, or until a toothpick or cake tester comes out clean. Set the pan on a wire rack to cool for at least 30 minutes.

7. Cut the brownies into 24 pieces while they are still in the pan. Carefully remove them with an offset spatula. Serve immediately, or let cool completely before covering with plastic wrap for storage at room temperature. They will stay fresh for up to 3 days. The brownies can be tightly wrapped in wax paper, sealed in a freezer-safe bag, and frozen for up to 2 months; allow them to thaw at room temperature before serving.

To vary this recipe
Whisk one of the following flavorings into the flour mixture:
1 tablespoon finely chopped candied ginger • 2 teaspoons grated lemon zest • 2 teaspoons ground cinnamon • 2 teaspoons finely minced fresh mint

and/or
Substitute one of the following liqueurs for the bourbon:
Amaretto or other almond-flavored liqueur • brandy • cognac • Calvados • Frangelico or other hazelnut-flavored liqueur • gold rum • Kahlúa or other coffee-flavored liqueur • spiced rum
and/or
Stir in 1¼ cups of any of the following mix-ins, or 1¼ cups any combination of the following mix-ins, with the flour mixture:
chocolate-covered espresso beans • chopped dried apples • chopped dried figs • chopped dried prunes • chopped honey-roasted almonds • chopped pecans • chopped walnuts • cocoa nibs • crumbled biscotti • dried cherries • semisweet chocolate chips.

Brown Sugar Brownies

Makes twenty-four 2¼ × 2⅛-inch brownies

As we tested brownies, these became the model for the others: sweet and rich, dense without being heavy, yet very chocolaty—a halfway point in the cake vs. fudge battle that plagues most brownie connoisseurs. Redolent of the molasses that's in the brown sugar, these brownies stand up well to heavier icings, such as Cocoa Frosting (page 153) or Milk Chocolate Buttercream (page 161).

1 cup all-purpose flour, plus additional for the pan
1 teaspoon baking powder
½ teaspoon salt
½ pound (2 sticks) unsalted butter, plus additional for the pan, at room temperature
5 ounces unsweetened chocolate, chopped
2 cups packed dark brown sugar
3 large eggs, at room temperature
2 teaspoons vanilla extract

1. Position the rack in the lower third of the oven. Preheat the oven to 350°F. Butter and flour a 9 × 13-inch baking pan; set it aside.

2. In a medium bowl, whisk the flour, baking powder, and salt until well combined. Set aside.

3. Place the butter and chocolate in the top of a double boiler set over simmering water. If you don't have a double boiler, place the butter and chocolate in a heat-safe bowl that fits snugly over a small pot of simmering water. Stir constantly until half the butter and chocolate is melted. Remove the top of the double boiler or the bowl from the pot; then continue stirring, away from the heat, until the butter and chocolate are completely melted. Transfer the mixture to a large bowl and allow to cool for 10 minutes. (To melt butter and chocolate in a microwave, see pages 9-10.)

4. Beat the brown sugar into the melted chocolate with a whisk or with an electric mixer at medium speed. Continue beating until the mixture is smooth and silky, about 6 minutes by hand or 3 minutes with a mixer. Beat in the eggs and vanilla just until incorporated.

5. With a wooden spoon or a rubber spatula, stir in the flour mixture just until combined. Do not beat. Spoon the batter into the prepared pan, spreading it gently to the corners.

6. Bake for 35 minutes, or until a toothpick or cake tester comes out with a few moist crumbs attached. Set the pan on a wire rack to cool for at least 30 minutes.

7. Cut the brownies into 24 pieces while they're still in the pan. Carefully remove them

with an offset spatula. Serve immediately, or let cool completely before covering with plastic wrap for storage at room temperature. They will stay fresh for up to 3 days. The brownies can be tightly wrapped in wax paper, sealed in a freezer-safe bag, and frozen for up to 2 months; allow them to thaw at room temperature before serving.

To vary this recipe
Whisk one of the following flavorings into the flour mixture:
1½ teaspoons ground cinnamon • 1½ teaspoons grated orange zest • 1 teaspoon ground ginger • 1 teaspoon pure chile powder

and/or
Add one of the following flavorings with the vanilla:
2 teaspoons bourbon • 1 teaspoon banana extract • 1 teaspoon butter flavoring • 1 teaspoon maple extract • 1 teaspoon raspberry extract • 1 teaspoon rum extract
and/or
Stir in ½ cup of any of the following mix-ins, or ½ cup any combination of the following mix-ins, with the flour mixture:
chopped banana chips • chopped candied chestnuts • chopped Heath bars • chopped toasted chickpeas • chopped Twix bars • dried cranberries • dried currants • mini marshmallows • white chocolate chips.

Brownie Cookies

Makes 24 cookies

Just once, we had to take the "bar" out of browine-making. These irresistibly dark chocolate treats have the taste of brownies but the texture of cookies: chewy in the middle, crunchy on the outside. Good on their own, they're also beautiful when iced with a thick white frosting, such as Marshmallow Cream Frosting (page 160) or Cream Cheese Frosting (page 155). Or serve them with a simple Lemon Curd alongside (page 159). Or use them as the tops and bottoms of truly magnificent ice cream sandwiches.

Unsalted butter, vegetable oil, or vegetable oil
  spray for the cookie sheets
1¼ cups all-purpose flour
½ cup unsweetened cocoa powder, sifted
½ teaspoon baking soda
½ teaspoon salt
10 tablespoons (1 stick plus 2 tablespoons)
  unsalted butter, at room temperature
1½ cups sugar
2 large eggs, at room temperature
1 tablespoon vanilla extract

1. Position the oven rack in the middle of the oven. Preheat the oven to 375°F. Lightly butter two 12 × 15-inch cookie sheets; alternatively, oil them with vegetable oil or a vegetable oil spray. Set them aside.

2. In a medium bowl, whisk the flour, cocoa powder, baking soda, and salt until well combined. Set aside.

3. In a large bowl, cream the butter and sugar with an electric mixer at medium speed. Continue beating until pale yellow and thick, about 5 minutes. Beat in the eggs and vanilla just until incorporated.

4. With a wooden spoon or a rubber spatula, stir in the flour mixture just until incorporated. Do not beat.

5. Drop the batter by tablespoonsful about 2½ inches apart onto the prepared cookie sheets, making about 12 cookies on each.

6. Cover one cookie sheet loosely with wax paper or a lint-free kitchen towel and set aside. Place the other sheet in the oven and bake for 9 minutes—the cookies should be slightly soft, not cracked or hard. Remove from the oven and allow to cool, on the cookie sheet, on a wire rack for 5 minutes. Meanwhile, uncover the unbaked cookies and bake for 9 minutes. Remove the partially cooled cookies from the sheet and allow them to cool completely on a rack. Remove the second cookie sheet from the oven and repeat the cooling process.

7. Serve immediately, or cover the cooled cookies with plastic wrap for storage at room temperature. They will stay fresh for about 2 days. The cookies may also be tightly wrapped in wax paper, sealed in a freezer-safe bag, and frozen for up to 2 months; allow them to thaw at room temperature before serving.

To vary this recipe

Whisk one or more of the following flavorings into the flour mixture:

2 teaspoons minced fresh basil leaves • 1 teaspoon ground cinnamon • 1 teaspoon minced fresh mint leaves • ½ teaspoon finely grated lemon zest

and/or

Substitute one of the following flavorings for the vanilla:

2 teaspoons maple extract • 1 teaspoon mint extract • 1 teaspoon almond extract

and/or

Stir in 1 cup of any of the following mix-ins, or 1 cup any combination of the following mix-ins, with the flour mixture:

chopped pecans • chopped toasted hazelnuts • cocoa nibs • dried currants • finely chopped dried apricots • mint chocolate chips • pinenuts • semisweet chocolate chips • unsalted shelled sunflower seeds • white chocolate chips.

Brownie Pancakes

Makes about twenty-four 4-inch pancakes

These light but chocolaty flapjacks are the perfect thing for a cold winter morning or a holiday breakfast. Serve them hot off the griddle, with lots of butter and warmed maple or blueberry syrup. Or serve them for dessert, topped with vanilla ice cream and hot fudge sauce.

1½ cups all-purpose flour
1 teaspoon baking soda
½ teaspoon salt
8 tablespoons (1 stick) unsalted butter, at room temperature
3 ounces unsweetened chocolate, chopped
3 large eggs, slightly beaten
⅔ cup sugar
1 teaspoon vanilla extract
1 cup milk (whole or low-fat, but not fat-free)

1. In a medium bowl, whisk the flour, baking soda, and salt until well combined. Set aside.

2. Place the butter and chocolate in the top of a double boiler set over simmering water. If you don't have a double boiler, place the butter and chocolate in a heat-safe bowl that fits snugly over a small pot of simmering water. Stir constantly until half the butter and chocolate is melted. Remove the top of the double boiler or the bowl from the pot; then continue stirring, away from the heat, until the butter and chocolate are completely melted. Transfer the mixture to a large bowl and allow to cool for 10 minutes. (To melt butter and chocolate in a microwave, see pages 9-10.)

3. Meanwhile, heat a nonstick griddle or a large nonstick skillet over medium-low heat.

4. In a large bowl, beat the eggs, sugar, and vanilla just until combined and foamy, using a whisk or an electric mixer at low speed. Beat in the melted chocolate mixture until the batter is uniform, about 4 minutes by hand or 2 minutes with a mixer.

5. With a wooden spoon or a rubber spatula, stir in the flour mixture just until combined; then stir in the milk just until the batter is pourable. Do not overmix. Pour 2 tablespoons of the batter onto the heated griddle; repeat, spacing the pancakes evenly. Cook 1 minute, until bubbles form across the surface of the pancakes; then turn, using a rubber spatula or other spatula safe for nonstick cookware. Cook an additional minute. Remove the pancakes from the griddle and serve immediately, or keep them warm on a cookie sheet or an ovenproof plate in a 250°F oven. Repeat with the remaining batter.

To vary this recipe

Stir in 1 cup of any of the following mix-ins, or 1 cup any combination of the following mix-ins, with the flour mixture:

chopped pecans • chopped walnuts • cocoa nibs • mint chocolate chips • shredded sweetened coconut • white chocolate chips

Serving Suggestions

- Allow the pancakes to cool and use them for the tops and bottoms of ice cream sandwiches.

- Layer the pancakes with sliced pears and drizzle the stack with warmed honey.
- Serve them with sour cream and shaved chocolate.
- Serve them hot with a sweetened sour cream made from 1 cup sour cream, 1 tablespoon sugar, and 1 teaspoon vanilla extract.
- Serve them with sweetened whipped cream and chopped nuts.

Brownie Waffles

Makes eight 8-inch waffles

Crunchy, delightful, and a real crowd-pleaser, these waffles will make your next breakfast a celebration. But don't stop there—some of the serving suggestions given below help you turn them into fantastic desserts as well.

½ cup plus 2 tablespoons solid vegetable
  shortening
4 ounces unsweetened chocolate, chopped
4 large eggs, at room temperature, lightly beaten
¾ cup plus 2 tablespoons sugar
2 teaspoons vanilla extract
1 teaspoon salt
2 cups all-purpose flour
1 cup milk (whole or low-fat, but not fat-free)

1. Place the shortening and chocolate in the top of a double boiler set over simmering water. If you don't have a double boiler, place the shortening and chocolate in a heat-safe bowl that fits snugly over a small pot of simmering water. Stir constantly until half the shortening and chocolate is melted. Remove the top of the double boiler or the bowl from the pot; then continue stirring, away from the heat, until the shortening and chocolate are completely melted. Allow to cool for no more than 3 minutes.

2. Meanwhile, heat and grease a waffle iron according to the manufacturer's instructions.

3. In a large bowl, beat the eggs, sugar, vanilla, and salt until smooth and well combined, using a whisk or an electric mixer at low speed. Slowly add the melted chocolate mixture in a thin ribbon, scraping down the sides of the bowl as necessary.

4. With a rubber spatula or a wooden spoon, stir ½ cup flour into the batter, then ½ cup milk, then ¾ cup flour, then the remaining ½ cup milk, and finally the remaining ¾ cup flour. Stir only until each addition is incorporated.

5. Pour ½ cup batter into the middle of the waffle iron. Close the lid and bake for 3 minutes or until the waffle is cooked to the desired crispness. Remove and repeat with the remaining batter. Serve the waffles immediately, or keep them warm on a cookie sheet or an oven-safe plate in a 250°F oven.

Serving Suggestions
- Serve them with sweetened whipped cream and Kahlúa or other coffee-flavored liqueur.
- Serve them with warmed honey rather than syrup.
- Use small pieces of the waffles to dip in a chocolate fondue.
- Use the waffles as the base for a new take on strawberry shortcake.

Brownies in a Jar

Makes 1 quart of brownie mix for one 9 × 13-inch pan of brownies

This is a great gift idea—a homemade brownie mix, layered beautifully in a quart-size Mason jar. Decorate the jar with stickers, wrap it in decorative paper, or tie a bow around the lid. You could also use a pretty fabric instead of a canning lid, securing the fabric with ribbon or with the screw-top ring of the traditional canning lid. You'll also need to include the brownie mix recipe card, given below the variations.

One 1-quart canning jar or 1-quart decorative jar, plus a lid
1½ teaspoons baking powder
1 teaspoon salt
1 cup all-purpose flour
¾ cup unsweetened cocoa powder, sifted
2 cups sugar
⅔ cup semisweet chocolate chips

1. Put the baking powder and salt in the jar. Carefully spoon the flour into the jar; gently tamp the flour down and wipe the inside of the jar with a dry paper towel to clean off any dust.

2. Carefully spoon in the cocoa powder, gently tamping it down and wiping down the inside of the jar with a clean dry paper towel.

3. Spoon the sugar into the jar, then add the chocolate chips. Seal the jar with a canning lid and ring or a decorative lid.

To vary this recipe

Substitute ⅔ cup of any of the following for the chocolate chips:
butterscotch chips • chopped toasted hazelnuts • chopped walnuts • cocoa nibs • dried blueberries • dried cranberries • M & M's • milk chocolate chips • mint chocolate chips • peanut butter chips • pinenuts • raisins • Reese's Pieces • white chocolate chips.

Brownie Mix Recipe Card

Preheat the oven to 350°F. Grease or butter and flour a 9 × 13-inch baking pan. Empty the brownie mix into a large bowl. Add ¾ cup unsalted butter or margarine, melted and cooled, and 4 large eggs, well beaten. Mix well and spread into the pan with a wooden spoon. Bake for 25 minutes or until a toothpick comes out with a few moist crumbs attached. Cool completely in the pan before cutting.

Burnt-Sugar Brownies

Makes twenty-four 2¼ × 2⅛-inch brownies

Mark's grandmother, Esther Rose Sophia Fain, worked for years as a pastry chef and used to make a meringue pie she called "burnt-sugar"—caramelized sugar infused into pastry cream, then poured into a short crust. To honor that recipe, we've melded "burnt sugar" with chocolate to create deep caramel brownies, sweet if still a tad sharp. They go perfectly with a cup of strong coffee or a glass of tawny Port.

1 cup all-purpose flour, plus additional for the pan
½ teaspoon baking powder
1 teaspoon salt
1½ cups sugar
⅓ cup boiling water
½ pound (2 sticks) unsalted butter, cut into
   1-tablespoon pieces, plus additional for the pan,
   at room temperature
6 ounces bittersweet or semisweet chocolate,
   chopped, or semisweet chocolate chips
4 ounces unsweetened chocolate, chopped
3 large eggs, at room temperature
1 tablespoon vanilla extract

1. Position the rack in the lower third of the oven. Preheat the oven to 350°F. Butter and flour a 9 × 13-inch baking pan; set it aside.

2. In a medium bowl, whisk the flour, baking powder, and salt until well combined. Set aside.

3. Melt the sugar in a heavy large saucepan over medium heat, stirring occasionally with a wooden spoon. Continue cooking and stirring until the sugar liquefies and caramelizes, turning dark amber, about 6 minutes. Immediately remove the pan from the heat and add the boiling water—be careful: the mixture will roil. Stir it down off the heat until a smooth caramel is formed.

4. Place the butter and both kinds of chocolate in a large bowl. Pour the hot caramel over them and stir constantly with a wooden spoon, until they are melted and the mixture is smooth, about 4 minutes.

5. In a medium bowl, beat the eggs until frothy with an electric mixer at medium speed. Beat a ladleful of the chocolate mixture into the eggs until smooth and uniform, about 1 minute. Then beat the egg mixture back into the chocolate mixture, scraping down the sides of the bowl as necessary. Continue beating until the mixture is smooth and silky, about 2 minutes. Stir in the vanilla.

6. With a wooden spoon or a rubber spatula, stir in the flour mixture just until combined. Do not beat. Spoon the batter into the prepared pan, spreading it gently to the corners.

7. Bake for 23 minutes, or until a toothpick or cake tester comes out with a few moist crumbs attached. Set the pan on a wire rack to cool for at least 30 minutes.

8. Cut the brownies into 24 pieces while they're still in the pan. Carefully remove them with an offset spatula. Serve immediately, or let cool completely before covering with plastic wrap for storage at room temperature. They will stay fresh for up to 3 days. The brownies can be tightly wrapped in wax paper, sealed in a freezer-safe bag, and frozen for up to 2 months; allow them to thaw at room temperature before serving.

To vary this recipe

Whisk one or more of the following spices into the flour mixture:

2 teaspoons ground cinnamon • 1½ teaspoons ground ginger • ½ teaspoon grated nutmeg *and/or*

Stir in 1¼ cups of any of the following mix-ins, or 1¼ cups any combination of the following mix-ins, with the flour mixture:

almond M & M's • chopped Heath bars • chopped Snickers bars • chopped toasted hazelnuts • chopped walnuts • dried cranberries • granola • mini marshmallows • raisins • semisweet chocolate chips.

Buttermilk Brownies

Makes twenty-four 2¼ × 2⅛-inch brownies

With one bite of these decadent treats, you'll experience the tangy taste of the old-fashioned buttermilk chocolate cakes that were so popular in the 1940s. If you're a fan of cakier brownies, don't rap the pan halfway through baking—the brownies will thus rise up higher and be far less dense.

1 cup all-purpose flour, plus additional for the pan
⅓ cup unsweetened cocoa powder, sifted
1 teaspoon salt
½ teaspoon baking powder
12 tablespoons (1½ sticks) unsalted butter, plus additional for the pan, at room temperature
4 ounces bittersweet or semisweet chocolate, chopped, or semisweet chocolate chips
3 ounces unsweetened chocolate, chopped
1½ cups sugar
2 large eggs, at room temperature
2 large egg yolks, at room temperature
1½ cups buttermilk (regular, low-fat, or fat-free)
2 teaspoons vanilla extract

1. Position the rack in the lower third of the oven. Preheat the oven to 350°F. Butter and flour a 9 × 13-inch baking pan; set it aside.

2. In a medium bowl, whisk the flour, cocoa powder, salt, and baking powder until well combined. Set aside.

3. Place the butter and both kinds of chocolate in the top of a double boiler set over simmering water. If you don't have a double boiler, place the butter and both kinds of chocolate in a heat-safe bowl that fits snugly over a small pot of simmering water. Stir constantly until half the butter and chocolate is melted. Remove the top of the double boiler or the bowl from the pot; then continue stirring, away from the heat, until the butter and chocolate are completely melted. Allow the mixture to cool for 10 minutes. (To melt butter and chocolate in a microwave, see pages 9-10.)

4. In a large bowl, beat the sugar, eggs, and egg yolks with an electric mixer at medium speed. Continue beating until the sugar has dissolved and the mixture is pale yellow and thick, about 6 minutes. Beat in the buttermilk and vanilla at low speed for 1 minute. Then beat in the chocolate mixture, scraping down the sides of the bowl as necessary. Continue beating until the mixture is uniform and smooth, about 3 minutes.

5. With a wooden spoon or a rubber spatula, stir in the flour mixture just until incorporated. Do not beat. Pour the batter into the prepared pan, spreading it gently to the corners.

6. Bake for 20 minutes, then rap the pan three or four times against the oven rack. Bake for an additional 15 minutes, or until a toothpick or cake tester comes out with a few moist crumbs attached. Set the pan on a wire rack to cool for at least 30 minutes.

7. Cut the brownies into 24 pieces while they're still in the pan. Carefully remove them with an offset spatula. Serve immediately, or let cool completely before covering with plastic wrap for storage at room temperature. They will stay fresh for up to 3 days. The brownies can be tightly wrapped in wax paper, sealed in a freezer-safe bag, and frozen for up to 3 months; allow them to thaw at room temperature before serving.

To vary this recipe
Whisk one or more of the following spices into the flour mixture:

2 tablespoons poppy seeds • 1 tablespoon chopped crystallized ginger • ½ teaspoon ground cloves
and/or
Substitute one of the following flavorings for the vanilla:
2 teaspoons almond extract • 1 teaspoon lemon extract • 1 teaspoon mint extract • 1 teaspoon maple extract
and/or
Stir in 1¼ cups of any of the following mix-ins, or 1¼ cups any combination of the following mix-ins, with the flour mixture:
butterscotch chips • chopped Butterfinger bars • chopped candied chestnuts • chopped caramels • chopped dates • chopped dried apples • chopped dried figs • chopped honey-roasted pecans • cocoa nibs • crumbled molasses cookies • peanut butter chips • semi-sweet chocolate chips.

Butterscotch Brownies

Makes sixteen 2¼ × 2¼-inch brownies

Chewy and rich, these brownies are like a Butterfinger bar turned into a cake. You might try a light icing like the classic Seven Minute Frosting (page 164) for a creamy taste, or Ganache Icing (page 157) for a much richer, more chocolate-intense treat.

1 cup all-purpose flour, plus additional for the pan
1 teaspoon baking powder
½ teaspoon salt
8 tablespoons (1 stick) unsalted butter, plus
　additional for the pan, at room temperature
1 cup butterscotch chips
⅔ cup packed light brown sugar
2 large eggs, at room temperature
½ cup unsweetened cocoa powder, sifted

1. Position the rack in the lower third of the oven. Preheat the oven to 350°F. Butter and flour a 9-inch square baking pan; set it aside.

2. In a medium bowl, whisk the flour, baking powder, and salt until well combined. Set aside.

3. Place the butter and butterscotch chips in the top of a double boiler set over simmering water. If you don't have a double boiler, place the butter and butterscotch chips in a heat-safe bowl that fits snugly over a small pot of simmer-

ing water. Stir constantly until half the butter and chips is melted. Remove the top of the double boiler or the bowl from the pot; then continue stirring, away from the heat, until the butter and chips are completely melted. Transfer to a large bowl and allow to cool for 10 minutes. The mixture may separate slightly—it will reincorporate in the next step.

4. Stir the brown sugar into the butterscotch mixture with a wooden spoon until the mixture is smooth, about 2 minutes. Beat in the eggs just until incorporated, using either a whisk or an electric mixer at medium speed. Beat in the cocoa powder, and continue beating until smooth, pale, and creamy, about 4 minutes by hand or 2 minutes with a mixer.

5. With a wooden spoon or a rubber spatula, stir in the flour mixture just until incorporated. Do not beat. Pour the batter into the prepared pan, spreading it gently to the corners.

6. Bake for 20 minutes, or until a toothpick or cake tester comes out with a few moist crumbs attached. Set the pan on a wire rack to cool for at least 30 minutes.

7. Cut the brownies into 16 squares while they're still in the pan. Carefully remove them

with an offset spatula. Serve immediately, or let cool completely before covering with plastic wrap for storage at room temperature. They will stay fresh for up to 3 days. The brownies can be tightly wrapped in wax paper, sealed in a freezer-safe bag, and frozen for up to 2 months; allow them to thaw at room temperature before serving.

To vary this recipe

Whisk one or more of the following flavorings into the flour mixture:

1 teaspoon grated orange zest • ½ teaspoon ground ginger • ½ teaspoon grated nutmeg

and/or

Add 1 teaspoon maple extract • or 1 teaspoon rum extract with the cocoa powder

and/or

Stir in ¾ cup of any of the following mix-ins, or ¾ cup any combination of the following mix-ins, with the flour mixture:

butterscotch chips • chopped candied chestnuts • chopped dried apricots • chopped pecans • chopped roasted unsalted peanuts • chopped walnuts • cocoa nibs • peanut butter chips • raisins • semisweet chocolate chips • slivered almonds • toasted pepitás • white chocolate chips.

Cake Brownies

Makes sixteen 2¼ × 2¼-inch brownies

These are the ultimate cake brownies. Fudge lovers, you'll have to skip ahead. These light cakey treats have an excellent crumb and they are light and delicate, but they don't skimp on chocolate at all. Since these brownies travel well, they're great for car trips and picnics. (Fingers, little or big, won't get messy.) But if you have lots of napkins handy, ice these delights with old-fashioned Buttercream (page 150).

1¼ cups all-purpose flour, plus additional for the pan

2 tablespoons unsweetened cocoa powder, sifted

1½ teaspoons baking powder

1 teaspoon salt

10 tablespoons (1 stick plus 2 tablespoons) unsalted butter, plus additional for the pan, at room temperature

4 ounces bittersweet or semisweet chocolate, chopped, or semisweet chocolate chips

2 large eggs, at room temperature

1 cup sugar

1½ teaspoons vanilla extract

1. Position the rack in the lower third of the oven. Preheat the oven to 350°F. Butter and flour a 9-inch square baking pan; set it aside.

2. In a medium bowl, whisk the flour, cocoa powder, baking powder, and salt until well combined. Set aside.

3. Place the butter and chocolate in the top of a double boiler set over simmering water. If you don't have a double boiler, place the butter and chocolate in a heat-safe bowl that fits snugly over a small pot of simmering water. Stir constantly until half the butter and chocolate is melted. Remove the top of the double boiler or the bowl from the pot; then continue stirring, away from the heat, until the butter and chocolate are completely melted. Allow to cool for 10 minutes. (To melt butter and chocolate in a microwave, see pages 9-10.)

4. In a large bowl, beat the eggs and sugar with an electric mixer at medium speed; continue beating until the mixture is pale yellow and thick, about 4 minutes. Beat in the vanilla and melted chocolate mixture until uniform and thick, about 2 minutes.

5. With a wooden spoon or a rubber spatula, stir in the flour mixture just until incorporated. Do not beat. Pour the batter into the prepared pan, spreading it gently to the corners.

6. Bake for 20 minutes, or until a toothpick or cake tester comes out with a few moist crumbs attached. Set the pan on a wire rack to cool for at least 30 minutes.

7. Cut the brownies into 16 squares while they're still in the pan. Carefully remove them

with an offset spatula. Serve immediately, or let cool completely before covering with plastic wrap for storage at room temperature. They will stay fresh for up to 2 days. The brownies can be tightly wrapped in wax paper, sealed in a freezer-safe bag, and frozen for up to 2 months; allow them to thaw at room temperature before serving.

To vary this recipe
Whisk one or more of the following spices into the flour mixture:
1½ teaspoons ground cinnamon • 1 teaspoon ground ginger • ½ teaspoon grated nutmeg • ½ teaspoon ground cloves
and/or
Substitute one of the following flavorings for the vanilla:
2 teaspoons spiced rum • 1 teaspoon almond extract • 1 teaspoon maple extract • 1 teaspoon orange extract
and/or
Stir in ¾ cup of any of the following mix-ins, or ¾ cup any combination of the following mix-ins, with the flour mixture:
chocolate-covered espresso beans • chopped dried apricots • chopped dried mango • chopped KitKat bars • chopped toasted hazelnuts • crumbled biscotti • crumbled Oreo cookies • dried blueberries • dried cranberries • granola • milk chocolate chips • mint chocolate chips • peanut butter chips • Raisinets • raisins • semisweet chocolate chips • shredded sweetened coconut • toasted pepitás • unsalted shelled sunflower seeds • white chocolate chips.

Chestnut Brownies

Makes twenty-four 2¼ × 2⅛-inch brownies

Chestnut purée is simply puréed chestnuts. Some brands do add sugar; unfortunately, they aren't directly labeled as such, so you have to read the ingredient list. For this recipe, use only unsweetened chestnut purée, which gives these brownies a smoother texture than other cakey brownies—almost like, well, a chestnut. Perfect for holidays, these brownies can be frosted with something simple like Chocolate Drizzle (page 151) or Vanilla Icing (page 166), or take them over the top with Ganache Icing (page 157).

½ cup all-purpose flour, plus additional for the pan
¼ cup unsweetened cocoa powder, sifted
1½ teaspoons baking powder
1 teaspoon salt
6 ounces bittersweet or semisweet chocolate, chopped, or semisweet chocolate chips
3 ounces unsweetened chocolate, chopped
½ pound (2 sticks) unsalted butter, plus additional for the pan, at room temperature
1½ cups sugar
One 15½-ounce can unsweetened chestnut purée
3 large eggs, at room temperature
2 teaspoons vanilla extract

1. Position the rack in the lower third of the oven. Preheat the oven to 350°F. Butter and flour a 9 × 13-inch baking pan; set it aside.

2. In a medium bowl, whisk the flour, cocoa powder, baking powder, and salt until well combined. Set aside.

3. Place both kinds of chocolate in the top of a double boiler set over simmering water. If you don't have a double boiler, place both kinds of chocolate in a heat-safe bowl that fits snugly over a small pot of simmering water. Stir constantly until half the chocolate is melted. Remove the top of the double boiler or the bowl from the pot; then continue stirring, away from the heat, until the chocolate is completely melted. Allow to cool for 5 minutes. (To melt chocolate in a microwave, see pages 9-10.)

4. In a large mixing bowl, cream the butter and sugar with an electric mixer at medium speed; continue beating until the mixture is pale yellow and thick, about 6 minutes. Beat in the chestnut purée, then the eggs one at a time, scraping down the sides of the bowl as necessary. Continue beating until the mixture is smooth and uniform, about 4 minutes. Beat in the vanilla and the chocolate mixture at low speed for 1 minute.

5. With a wooden spoon or a rubber spatula, stir in the flour mixture just until incorporated.

Do not beat. Spoon the batter into the prepared pan, spreading it gently to the corners.

6. Bake for 35 minutes, or until a toothpick or cake tester comes out with a few moist crumbs attached. Set the pan on a wire rack to cool for about 30 minutes.

7. Cut the brownies into 24 pieces while they're still in the pan. Carefully remove them with an offset spatula. Serve immediately, or let cool completely before covering with plastic wrap for storage at room temperature. They will stay fresh for up to 3 days. The brownies may be wrapped tightly in wax paper, sealed in a freezer-safe bag, and frozen for up to 2 months; allow them to thaw at room temperature before serving.

To vary this recipe
Whisk one of the following flavorings into the flour mixture:
1½ tablespoons poppy seeds • 2 teaspoons chopped crystallized ginger • 2 teaspoons bourbon • 1½ teaspoons ground cinnamon • 1 teaspoon ground black pepper • 1 teaspoon ground cardamom • 1 teaspoon ground thyme • 1 teaspoon ground sage

and/or
Add 1½ teaspoons maple extract • or 1½ teaspoons rum extract with the vanilla
and/or
Stir in 1¼ cups of any of the following mix-ins, or 1¼ cups any combination of the following mix-ins, with the flour mixture:
chopped candied chestnuts • chopped dates • chopped dried apples • chopped honey-roasted walnuts • crumbled gingersnap cookies • dried cherries • dried cranberries • semisweet chocolate chips.

Chile Brownies

Makes twenty-four 2¼ × 2⅛-inch brownies

A staple in some Texas bakeries, Chile Brownies are spicy and sweet, a combination perhaps unfamiliar to, well, other folks (aka Yankees). While kids might prefer simpler brownies, these have a peppery kick many grown-ups adore. We didn't skimp on the chocolate by an ounce. These brownies would be perfect after a barbecue dinner, a fajita supper, or a chili cook-off.

¾ cup all-purpose flour, plus additional for the pan
¼ cup plus 1 tablespoon pure chile powder (see page 5)
1 teaspoon baking powder
1 teaspoon salt
12 tablespoons (1½ sticks) unsalted butter, plus additional for the pan, at room temperature
5 ounces bittersweet or semisweet chocolate, chopped, or semisweet chocolate chips
5 ounces unsweetened chocolate, chopped
1¼ cups sugar
3 large eggs, at room temperature

1. Position the rack in the lower third of the oven. Preheat the oven to 350°F. Butter and flour a 9 × 13-inch baking pan; set it aside.

2. In a medium bowl, whisk the flour, chile powder, baking powder, and salt until well combined. Set aside.

3. Place the butter and both kinds of chocolate in the top of a double boiler set over simmering water. If you don't have a double boiler, place the butter and both kinds of chocolate in a heatsafe bowl that fits snugly over a small pot of simmering water. Stir constantly until half the butter and chocolate is melted. Remove the top of the double boiler or the bowl from the pot; then continue stirring, away from the heat, until the butter and chocolate are completely melted. Transfer to a large bowl and allow to cool for 10 minutes. (To melt chocolate and butter in a microwave, see pages 9-10.)

4. Beat the sugar into the melted chocolate mixture with a whisk or with an electric mixer at medium speed; continue beating until smooth and silky, about 5 minutes by hand or 2 minutes with a mixer. Beat in the eggs until well incorporated.

5. With a wooden spoon or a rubber spatula, stir in the flour mixture just until incorporated. Do not beat. Spoon the batter into the prepared pan, spreading it gently to the corners.

6. Bake for 20 minutes, or until a toothpick or cake tester comes out with a few moist crumbs attached. Set the pan on a wire rack to cool for at least 30 minutes.

7. Cut the brownies into 24 pieces while they're still in the pan. Carefully remove them with an offset spatula. Serve immediately, or let cool completely before covering with plastic wrap for storage at room temperature. They will stay fresh for up to 3 days. The brownies can be tightly wrapped in wax paper, sealed in a freezer-safe bag, and frozen for up to 2 months; allow them to thaw at room temperature before serving.

To vary this recipe
Add one or more of the following spices with the chile powder:
1½ tablespoons ground cinnamon • 2 teaspoons ground ginger • 1 teaspoon grated nutmeg • 1 teaspoon ground cloves

and/or
Stir in 1¼ cups of any of the following mix-ins, or 1¼ cups any combination of the following mix-ins, with the flour mixture:
chocolate-covered espresso beans • chopped banana chips • chopped candied chestnuts • chopped candied orange peel • chopped dried figs • chopped dried papaya • chopped dried prunes • chopped pecans • chopped toasted chickpeas • chopped toasted hazelnuts • chopped unsalted roasted peanuts • crumbled biscotti • dried cherries • Goobers • raisins • toasted pepitás.

Chocolate Syrup Brownies

Makes sixteen 2¼ × 2¼-inch brownies

Although somewhat out of vogue today, Chocolate Syrup Brownies were among the first chocolate brownies to come into style in the 1920s. Chocolate syrup had come out of the malt shops and gone straight to home kitchens, thanks to the advent of home refrigeration. Since chocolate syrup fast became a national craze, it naturally showed up in brownies, that other Jazz Age craze. These old-fashioned treats are so simple, so sweet, that with one bite you'll know they'll never be out of style in your home.

1 cup all-purpose flour, plus additional for the pan
½ teaspoon baking powder
½ teaspoon salt
10 tablespoons (1 stick plus 2 tablespoons) unsalted butter, plus additional for the pan, at room temperature
⅔ cup sugar
1 cup chocolate syrup
2 teaspoons vanilla extract
2 large eggs, at room temperature

1. Position the rack in the lower third of the oven. Preheat the oven to 350°F. Butter and flour a 9-inch square baking pan; set it aside.

2. In a medium bowl, whisk the flour, baking powder, and salt until well combined. Set aside.

3. In a large bowl, cream the butter and sugar with a wooden spoon or with an electric mixer at medium speed. Continue beating until the mixture is smooth and silky, about 6 minutes by hand or 3 minutes with a mixer. Beat in the chocolate syrup and vanilla, then the eggs, just until incorporated.

4. With a wooden spoon or a rubber spatula, stir in the flour mixture just until incorporated. Do not beat. Pour the batter into the prepared pan, spreading it gently to the corners.

5. Bake for 30 minutes, or until a toothpick or cake tester comes out dry. Set the pan on a wire rack to cool for at least 30 minutes.

6. Cut the brownies into 16 squares while they're still in the pan. Carefully remove them with an offset spatula. Serve immediately, or let cool completely before covering with plastic wrap for storage at room temperature. They will stay fresh for up to 4 days. The brownies can also be tightly wrapped in wax paper, sealed in a freezer-safe bag, and frozen for up to 3 months; allow them to thaw at room temperature before serving.

To vary this recipe
Whisk one or more of the following flavorings into the flour mixture:

1 teaspoon grated lemon zest • 1 teaspoon grated orange zest • ½ teaspoon grated nutmeg
and/or
Add one of the following flavorings with the vanilla:
1 tablespoon crème de cassis • 1 teaspoon banana extract • 1 teaspoon coffee extract • 1 teaspoon maple extract • 1 teaspoon mint extract • 1 teaspoon rum extract
and/or
Stir in ¾ cup of any of the following mix-ins, or ¾ cup any combination of the following mix-ins, with the flour mixture:

chopped dried apricots • chopped dried prunes • chopped Heath bars • chopped honey-roasted peanuts • chopped pecans • chopped Peppermint Patties • chopped walnuts • crumbled pecan sandy cookies • dried currants • peanut butter chips • Reese's Pieces • slivered almonds • white chocolate chips • yellow raisins.

Cocoa Brownies

Makes twenty-four $2\frac{1}{4} \times 2\frac{1}{8}$-inch brownies

The only chocolate in these brownies is unsweetened cocoa powder, but they're still thick, dense, and surprisingly fudgy. If you want them even fudgier, reduce the baking time by 3 minutes and let them cool for at least 2 hours before cutting. They're also good right out of the freezer: cold, chewy, and very chocolaty. Smear frozen ones with Ganache Icing (page 157) and you'll swear you're eating a candy bar.

1 cup all-purpose flour, plus additional for the pan
¾ cup unsweetened cocoa powder, sifted
½ teaspoon baking powder
½ teaspoon salt
½ pound (2 sticks) unsalted butter, plus additional for the pan, at room temperature
2 cups sugar
4 large eggs, at room temperature
2 teaspoons vanilla extract

1. Position the rack in the lower third of the oven. Preheat the oven to 350°F. Butter and flour a 9 × 13-inch baking pan; set it aside.

2. In a medium bowl, whisk the flour, cocoa powder, baking powder, and salt until well combined. Set aside.

3. In a large bowl, cream the butter and sugar with an electric mixer at medium speed; continue beating until pale yellow and thick, about 5 minutes. Beat in the eggs one at a time, making sure each is thoroughly incorporated before adding the next. After beating in the fourth egg for 1 minute, stir in the vanilla.

4. With a wooden spoon or a rubber spatula, stir in the flour mixture just until combined. Do not beat, although the batter will be quite thick. Spoon the batter into the prepared pan, spreading it gently to the corners.

5. Bake for 27 minutes, or until a toothpick or cake tester comes out dry. Set the pan on a wire rack to cool for at least 1 hour. The cake may fall at its center.

6. Cut the brownies into 24 pieces while they're still in the pan. Carefully remove them with an offset spatula. Serve immediately, or let cool completely before covering with plastic wrap for storage at room temperature. They will stay fresh for up to 3 days. The brownies can be tightly wrapped in wax paper, sealed in a freezer-safe bag, and frozen for up to 2 months; allow them to thaw at room temperature before serving.

To vary this recipe

Whisk one or more of the following spices into the flour mixture:

2 teaspoons ground cinnamon • 1½ teaspoons ground cloves • ½ teaspoon grated nutmeg

and/or

Decrease the flour to ¾ cup and add ¼ cup finely ground almonds

and/or

Stir 1¼ cups of any of the following mix-ins, or 1¼ cups any combination of the following mix-ins, with the flour mixture:

butterscotch chips • cocoa nibs • chopped Baby Ruth bars • chopped KitKat bars • chopped pecans • plain or chocolate-covered espresso beans • granola • milk chocolate chips • mint chocolate chips • raspberry chocolate chips • pinenuts • raisins • unsalted shelled sunflower seeds • white chocolate chips.

Cocoa Nib Brownies

Makes sixteen 2¼ × 2¼-inch brownies

These fudgy brownies are made with the essence of chocolate: cocoa nibs. Although they are delicious on their own, we ask you to grind the nibs to release their distinctive flavor into the batter; grind them only until they are like sea salt, not a powder. Depending on the size of your grinder, you may have to do this in batches. To avoid cross-pollinating spices and flavors in your grinder, clean it between uses by processing 1 tablespoon raw rice until it's a fine powder, then discarding the ground rice and thoroughly wiping out the grinder.

½ cup all-purpose flour, plus additional for the pan
½ teaspoon baking powder
½ teaspoon salt
8 tablespoons (1 stick) unsalted butter, plus
  additional for the pan, at room temperature
8 ounces bittersweet or semisweet chocolate,
  chopped, or semisweet chocolate chips
1 cup sugar
2 large eggs, at room temperature
2 teaspoons vanilla extract
¾ cup cocoa nibs (see page 7), coarsely ground in
  a spice grinder or a coffee grinder

1. Position the rack in the lower third of the oven. Preheat the oven to 350°F. Butter and flour a 9-inch square baking pan; set it aside.

2. In a medium bowl, whisk the flour, baking powder, and salt until well combined. Set aside.

3. Place the butter and chocolate in the top of a double boiler set over simmering water. If you don't have a double boiler, place the butter and chocolate in a heat-safe bowl that fits snugly over a small pot of simmering water. Stir constantly until half the butter and chocolate is melted. Remove the top of the double boiler or the bowl from the pot; then continue stirring, away from the heat, until the butter and chocolate are completely melted. Transfer the mixture to a large bowl and allow to cool for 10 minutes. (To melt butter and chocolate in a microwave, see pages 9-10.)

4. Beat the sugar into the melted chocolate with a whisk or with an electric mixer at medium speed; continue beating until the mixture is smooth and silky, about 6 minutes by hand or 3 minutes with a mixer. Beat in the eggs one at a time, adding the second only after the first is thoroughly incorporated. After beating in the second egg for 1 minute, beat in the vanilla.

5. With a wooden spoon or a rubber spatula, stir in the nibs and the flour mixture just until incorporated. Do not beat. Pour the batter into the prepared pan, spreading it gently to the corners.

6. Bake for 20 minutes, or until a toothpick or cake tester comes out with a few moist crumbs attached. Set the pan on a wire rack to cool for at least 30 minutes.

7. Cut the brownies into 16 squares while they're still in the pan. Carefully remove them with an offset spatula. Serve immediately, or let cool completely before covering with plastic wrap for storage at room temperature. They will stay fresh for up to 3 days. The brownies can be tightly wrapped in wax paper, sealed in a freezer-safe bag, and frozen for up to 3 months; allow them to thaw at room temperature before serving.

To vary this recipe
Whisk one of the following spices into the flour mixture:
2 teaspoons pure chile powder • 2 teaspoons poppy seeds • 1 teaspoon ground cinnamon • 1 teaspoon ground ginger

and/or
Substitute one of the following flavorings for the vanilla:
1 teaspoon coffee extract • 1 teaspoon coconut extract • 1 teaspoon maple extract • 1 teaspoon rum extract

and/or
Stir in ¾ cup of any of the following mix-ins, or ¾ cup any combination of the following mix-ins, with the flour mixture:
chocolate-covered espresso beans • chopped dates • chopped Heath bars • chopped honey-roasted almonds • chopped unsalted roasted peanuts • dried currants • mini marshmallows • mint chocolate chips • Raisinets • Reese's Pieces • semisweet chocolate chips.

Coconut Brownies

Makes sixteen 2¼ × 2¼-inch brownies

Coconut lovers, here's your fix. These intense brownies are wonderfully chewy, partly because they are made with both unsweetened coconut flakes and sweetened cream of coconut. The first is sold in some gourmet markets and in most health-food stores—it is not sweetened baking coconut. The second is used in blender drinks and is sold in the drinks aisle of most supermarkets—it is not coconut milk. Coconut Brownies are quite rich—and so probably work well on their own, unfrosted.

½ cup all-purpose flour, plus additional for the pan
½ cup unsweetened cocoa powder, sifted
½ teaspoon baking powder
½ teaspoon salt
8 tablespoons (1 stick) unsalted butter, plus
   additional for the pan, at room temperature
¾ cup sugar
½ cup sweetened cream of coconut
2 large eggs, at room temperature
1 teaspoon vanilla extract
½ cup unsweetened coconut flakes

1. Position the rack in the lower third of the oven. Preheat the oven to 350°F. Butter and flour a 9-inch square baking pan; set it aside.

2. In a medium bowl, whisk the flour, cocoa powder, baking powder, and salt. Set aside.

3. In a large bowl, cream the butter, sugar, and cream of coconut with a wooden spoon or with an electric mixer at medium speed. Continue beating until smooth and uniform, about 8 minutes by hand or 3 minutes with a mixer. Beat in the eggs and vanilla just until incorporated.

4. With a wooden spoon or a rubber spatula, stir in the coconut flakes and the flour mixture just until incorporated. Do not beat. Pour the batter into the prepared pan, spreading it gently to the corners.

5. Bake for 20 minutes, or until a toothpick or cake tester comes out with a few moist crumbs attached. Set the pan on a wire rack to cool for at least 30 minutes.

6. Cut the brownies into 16 squares while they're still in the pan. Carefully remove them with an offset spatula. Serve immediately, or let cool completely before covering with plastic wrap for storage at room temperature. They will stay fresh for up to 4 days. The brownies can also be tightly wrapped in wax paper, sealed in a freezer-safe bag, and frozen for up to 2 months; allow them to thaw at room temperature before serving.

To vary this recipe

Whisk 1 teaspoon ground ginger into the flour mixture

and/or

Substitute one of the following flavorings for the vanilla:

1½ teaspoons banana extract • 1 teaspoon almond extract • 1 teaspoon rum extract

and/or

Stir in ¾ cup of any of the following mix-ins, or ¾ cup any combination of the following mix-ins, with the flour mixture:

butterscotch chips • chopped banana chips • chopped candied chestnuts • chopped Heath bars • chopped honey-roasted peanuts • chopped PayDay bars • chopped pecans • chopped Twix bars • cocoa nibs • crumbled Oreo cookies • peanut butter chips • raisins • semisweet chocolate chips • slivered almonds • white chocolate chips.

Coffee Brownies

Makes twenty-four 2¼ × 2⅛-inch brownies

If you enjoy a cup of coffee with a brownie, look no further for the easiest way to have both at once. You can frost these delights with Seven Minute Frosting (page 164) or Ganache Icing (page 157), or you can really wake up your tastebuds with Mocha Cream Frosting (page 162).

¼ cup instant coffee powder

2 tablespoons hot water

⅔ cup all-purpose flour, plus additional for the pan

2 tablespoons unsweetened cocoa powder, sifted

½ teaspoon baking soda

½ teaspoon salt

12 tablespoons (1½ sticks) unsalted butter, plus additional for the pan, at room temperature

6 ounces bittersweet or semisweet chocolate, chopped, or semisweet chocolate chips

4 large eggs, at room temperature

1⅓ cups sugar

1 teaspoon vanilla extract

1. In a small bowl, stir the coffee powder and hot water until the powder is thoroughly dissolved and the mixture is smooth, about 1 minute. Set aside to cool.

2. Position the rack in the lower third of the oven. Preheat the oven to 350°F. Butter and flour a 9 × 13-inch baking pan; set it aside.

3. In a medium bowl, whisk the flour, cocoa powder, baking soda, and salt until well combined. Set aside.

4. Place the butter and chocolate in the top of a double boiler set over simmering water. If you don't have a double boiler, place the butter and chocolate in a heat-safe bowl that fits snugly over a small pot of simmering water. Stir constantly until half the butter and chocolate is melted. Remove the top of the double boiler or the bowl from the pot; then continue stirring, away from the heat, until the chocolate and butter are completely melted. In a slow thin stream, stirring all the while, pour in the coffee mixture; stir until the mixture is smooth and uniform, about 2 minutes. Allow to cool for 10 minutes. (To melt butter and chocolate in a microwave, see pages 9-10.)

5. In a large bowl, beat the eggs, sugar, and vanilla with an electric mixer at medium speed; continue beating until pale yellow and thick, about 6 minutes. Slowly pour in the chocolate mixture, beating all the while at medium speed and scraping down the sides of the bowl as necessary. Continue beating until the mixture is smooth, about 2 minutes.

6. With a wooden spoon or a rubber spatula, stir in the flour mixture just until incorporated.

Do not beat. Pour the batter into the prepared pan, spreading it gently to the corners.

7. Bake for 25 minutes, or until a toothpick or cake tester comes out with a few moist crumbs attached. Set the pan on a wire rack to cool for at least 30 minutes.

8. Cut the brownies into 24 pieces while they're still in the pan. Carefully remove them with an offset spatula. Serve immediately, or let cool completely before covering with plastic wrap for storage at room temperature. They will stay fresh for up to 3 days. The brownies may be tightly wrapped in wax paper, sealed in a freezer-safe bag, and frozen for up to 3 months; allow them to thaw at room temperature before serving.

To vary this recipe
Whisk one of the following spices into the flour mixture:
1 tablespoon poppy seeds • 2 teaspoons ground cinnamon • 1 teaspoon ground cardamom • 1 teaspoon ground mace

and/or
Substitute instant espresso powder for the instant coffee
and/or
Substitute 1 teaspoon almond extract • or 1 teaspoon rum extract for the vanilla:
and/or
Stir in 1¼ cups of any of the following mix-ins, or 1¼ cups any combination of the following mix-ins, with the flour mixture:
almond M & M's • chocolate-covered espresso beans • chopped Butterfinger bars • chopped dried apples • chopped dried apricots • chopped dried prunes • chopped Heath bars • chopped pecans • chopped toasted hazelnuts • chopped unsalted roasted peanuts • milk chocolate chips • semisweet chocolate chips • slivered almonds • white chocolate chips.

Cola Brownies

Makes twenty-four 2¼ × 2⅛-inch brownies

A Southern favorite, cola cake has graced many a family reunion. Here we've transformed this standard into brownies—they are quite cakey, to honor the original. If you want fudgier brownies, rap the pan three or four times on the oven rack after 20 minutes' baking time, then continue baking as directed. Of course, there's only one icing: Cola Icing (page 154).

1½ cups all-purpose flour, plus additional for the pan
1 teaspoon baking soda
1 teaspoon salt
10 ounces bittersweet or semisweet chocolate, chopped, or semisweet chocolate chips
½ pound (2 sticks) unsalted butter, plus additional for the pan, at room temperature
1 cup sugar
3 large eggs, at room temperature
1 cup carbonated cola
1 teaspoon vanilla extract

1. Position the rack in the lower third of the oven. Preheat the oven to 350°F. Butter and flour a 9 × 13-inch baking pan; set it aside.

2. In a medium bowl, whisk the flour, baking soda, and salt until well combined. Set aside.

3. Place the chocolate in the top of a double boiler set over simmering heat. If you don't have a double boiler, place the chocolate in a heat-safe bowl that fits snugly over a small pot of simmering water. Stir constantly until half the chocolate is melted. Remove the top of the double boiler or the bowl from the pot; then continue stirring, away from the heat, until the chocolate is completely melted. Allow to cool for 5 minutes. (To melt chocolate in a microwave, see pages 9-10.)

4. In a large bowl, cream the butter and sugar with an electric mixer at medium speed; continue beating until pale yellow and thick, about 6 minutes. Beat in the eggs one at a time, allowing each to be thoroughly incorporated before adding the next. After beating in the third egg for 1 minute, add the melted chocolate, beating constantly for 2 minutes and scraping down the sides of the bowl as necessary.

5. With a wooden spoon or a rubber spatula, stir in the flour mixture just until incorporated. Gently stir in the cola and vanilla; then pour the batter into the prepared pan, spreading it gently to the corners.

6. Bake for 35 minutes, or until a toothpick or cake tester comes out clean. Set the pan on a wire rack to cool for at least 30 minutes.

7. Cut the brownies into 24 pieces while they're still in the pan. Carefully remove them with an offset spatula. Serve immediately, or let cool completely before covering with plastic wrap for storage at room temperature. They will stay fresh for up to 2 days. The brownies can also be tightly wrapped in wax paper, sealed in a freezer-safe bag, and frozen for up to 3 months; allow them to thaw at room temperature before serving.

To vary this recipe
Whisk one or more of the following spices into the flour mixture:
2 teaspoons ground cinnamon • ½ teaspoon grated nutmeg • ½ teaspoon ground cloves

and/or
Substitute one of the following for the cola:
cherry cola • cream soda • ginger beer • root beer
and/or
Stir in 1¼ cups of any of the following mix-ins, or 1¼ cups any combination of the following mix-ins, with the flour mixture:
chopped Baby Ruth bars • chopped caramels • chopped dates • chopped pecans • chopped toasted hazelnuts • chopped walnuts • crumbled molasses cookies • dried blueberries • dried cherries • milk chocolate chips • mini marshmallows • peanut butter chips • peanut M & M's • semisweet chocolate chips • shredded sweetened coconut.

Cornbread Brownies

Makes sixteen 2 × 2-inch brownies

The rather unusual combination of corn and cocoa is actually a tradition among indigenous Central American peoples. The cornmeal gives these fudgy brownies a grainy, crunchy texture, somewhat like ground cocoa nibs, only sweeter. A bit more sophisticated than the run-of-the-mill brownie, Cornbread Brownies make a great dessert after a Southwestern meal—and an even better breakfast the next morning.

½ cup finely ground yellow cornmeal
½ cup unsweetened cocoa powder, sifted
¼ cup all-purpose flour, plus additional for the pan
1 teaspoon salt
½ teaspoon baking powder
1 cup sugar
½ cup corn oil or vegetable oil, plus additional for the pan
2 large eggs, at room temperature
1 teaspoon vanilla extract

1. Position the rack in the lower third of the oven. Preheat the oven to 350°F. Oil and flour an 8-inch square baking pan; set it aside.

2. In a medium bowl, whisk the cornmeal, cocoa powder, flour, salt, and baking powder until well combined. Set aside.

3. In a large mixing bowl, beat the sugar and oil with an electric mixer at medium speed; continue beating until smooth and silky, about 4 minutes. Beat in the eggs one at a time, allowing the first to be thoroughly incorporated before adding the second. After beating in the second egg for 1 minute, add the vanilla.

4. With a wooden spoon or a rubber spatula, stir in the flour mixture just until incorporated. Do not beat. Spoon the batter into the prepared pan, spreading it gently to the corners.

5. Bake for 25 minutes. A toothpick will come out wet, and the top will still be soft—the brownies will set as they cool. Set the pan on a wire rack to cool for at least 1 hour.

6. Cut the brownies into 16 squares while they're still in the pan. Carefully remove them with an offset spatula. Serve immediately, or let cool completely before covering with plastic wrap for storage at room temperature. They will stay fresh for up to 2 days. The brownies can be tightly wrapped in wax paper, sealed in a freezer-safe bag, and frozen for up to 2 months; allow them to thaw at room temperature before serving.

To vary this recipe

Whisk one of the following flavorings into the flour mixture:

1 teaspoon grated lemon zest • 1 teaspoon ground cinnamon • 1 teaspoon ground ginger • 1 teaspoon minced thyme

and/or

Stir in ½ cup of any of the following mix-ins, or ½ cup any combination of the following mix-ins, with the flour mixture:

chopped dried apples • chopped dried mango • chopped toasted chickpeas • chopped walnuts • dried cherries • raisins • semisweet chocolate chips • slivered almonds • unsalted shelled sunflower seeds.

Cranberry Brownies

Makes twenty-four 2¼ × 2⅛-inch brownies

When we set about testing a cranberry brownie, we found that dried cranberries were too subtle and fresh berries were just too tart. The solution? Cranberry sauce, that Thanksgiving staple. Use whole cranberry sauce, not the jellied version that comes out of the can in one loaf. These brownies are perfect when you're tired of the usual but don't want to go too far out on a limb.

1⅓ cups all-purpose flour, plus additional
   for the pan
1 teaspoon baking powder
½ teaspoon salt
8 tablespoons (1 stick) unsalted butter, plus
   additional for the pan, at room temperature
5 ounces bittersweet or semisweet chocolate,
   chopped, or semisweet chocolate chips
3 ounces unsweetened chocolate, chopped
2 large eggs, at room temperature
1¼ cups sugar
One 16-ounce can whole-berry cranberry sauce
½ teaspoon almond extract

1. Position the rack in the lower third of the oven. Preheat the oven to 350°F. Butter and flour a 9 × 13-inch baking pan; set it aside.

2. In a medium bowl, whisk the flour, baking powder, and salt until well combined. Set aside.

3. Place the butter and both kinds of chocolate in the top of a double boiler set over simmering water. If you don't have a double boiler, place the butter and both kinds of chocolate in a heat-safe bowl that fits snugly over a small pot of simmering water. Stir constantly until half the butter and chocolate is melted. Remove the top of the double boiler or the bowl from the pot; then continue stirring, away from the heat, until the butter and chocolate are completely melted. Allow to cool for 10 minutes. (To melt butter and chocolate in a microwave, see pages 9-10.)

4. In a large bowl, beat the eggs and sugar with an electric mixer at medium speed; continue beating until the sugar has dissolved and the mixture is thick, about 5 minutes. Beat in the cranberry sauce, almond extract, and chocolate mixture until smooth, about 4 minutes, scraping down the sides of the bowl as necessary.

5. With a wooden spoon or a rubber spatula, stir in the flour mixture just until incorporated. Do not beat. Pour the batter into the prepared pan, spreading it gently to the corners.

6. Bake for 25 minutes, or until a toothpick or cake tester comes out clean. Set the pan on a wire rack to cool for at least 30 minutes.

7. Cut the brownies into 24 pieces while they're still in the pan. Carefully remove them with an offset spatula. Serve immediately, or let them cool completely before covering with plastic wrap for storage at room temperature. They will stay fresh for up to 3 days. The brownies can also be tightly wrapped in wax paper, sealed in a freezer-safe bag, and frozen for up to 2 months; allow them to thaw at room temperature before serving.

To vary this recipe
Add one or more of the following spices to the flour mixture:
1½ teaspoons ground ginger • ½ teaspoon ground cloves • ½ teaspoon grated nutmeg

and/or
Stir in 1¼ cups of any of the following mix-ins, or 1¼ cups any combination of the following mix-ins, with the flour mixture:
chocolate-covered espresso beans • chopped candied orange peel • chopped dried figs • chopped dried pineapple • chopped pecans • chopped toasted hazelnuts • dried cherries • dried currants • granola • pinenuts • raisins • unsalted shelled sunflower seeds.

Cream Cheese Brownies

Makes twenty-four 2¼ × 2⅛-inch brownies

Call it a New York weakness, but we had to make a brownie that crossed cheesecake with fudge. The result was this decadent treat: creamy, a little tart, but very fudgy. As a bonus, these brownies are great right out of the freezer, like frozen candy bars. If you really want to load it on, ice them with Chocolate Fudge Frosting (page 152) or Five Minute Chocolate Frosting (page 156).

2 cups all-purpose flour, plus additional for the pan

½ teaspoon baking powder

½ teaspoon salt

4 ounces bittersweet or semisweet chocolate, chopped, or semisweet chocolate chips

4 ounces unsweetened chocolate, chopped

10 tablespoons (1 stick plus 2 tablespoons) unsalted butter, plus additional for the pan, at room temperature

8 ounces cream cheese, softened

1¾ cups sugar

4 large eggs, at room temperature

1 egg yolk, at room temperature

1 tablespoon vanilla extract

1. Position the rack in the lower third of the oven. Preheat the oven to 350°F. Butter and flour a 9 × 13-inch baking pan; set it aside.

2. In a medium bowl, whisk the flour, baking powder, and salt until well combined. Set aside.

3. Place both kinds of chocolate in the top of a double boiler set over simmering water. If you don't have a double boiler, place both kinds of chocolate in a heat-safe bowl that fits snugly over a small pot of simmering water. Stir constantly until the half the chocolate is melted. Remove the top of the double boiler or the bowl from the pot; then continue stirring, away from the heat, until the chocolate is completely melted. Allow to cool for 5 minutes. (To melt chocolate in a microwave, see pages 9-10.)

4. In a large bowl, cream the butter, cream cheese, and sugar with an electric mixer at medium speed; continue beating until the sugar has dissolved and the mixture is thick and smooth, about 5 minutes. Beat in the melted chocolate until smooth and uniform, about 2 minutes, scraping down the sides of the bowl as necessary. Beat in the eggs one at a time, beating each in thoroughly before adding the next. Beat in the egg yolk and vanilla.

5. With a wooden spoon or a rubber spatula, stir in the flour mixture just until incorporated. Do not beat. Pour the batter into the prepared pan, spreading it gently to the corners.

6. Bake for 25 minutes, or until a toothpick or cake tester comes out with a few moist crumbs attached. The middle may be soft but it should be set. Set the pan on a wire rack to cool for at least 1 hour.

7. Cut the brownies into 24 pieces while they're still in the pan. Carefully remove them with an offset spatula. Serve immediately, or let cool completely before covering with plastic wrap for storage at room temperature. They will stay fresh for up to 4 days. The brownies can also be tightly wrapped in wax paper, sealed in a freezer-safe bag, and frozen for up to 4 months; allow them to thaw at room temperature before serving.

To vary this recipe
Whisk one of the following flavorings into the flour mixture:
2 tablespoons poppy seeds • 1 tablespoon chopped crystallized ginger • 2 teaspoons ground cinnamon • 1½ teaspoons finely grated lemon zest

and/or
Substitute one of the following flavorings for the vanilla:
2 teaspoons banana extract • 1½ teaspoons almond extract • 1½ teaspoons coconut extract • 1½ teaspoons mint extract • 1½ teaspoons rum extract

and/or
Stir in 1¼ cups of any of the following mix-ins, or 1¼ cups any combination of the following mix-ins, with the flour mixture:
chocolate-covered espresso beans • chopped dates • chopped dried apricots • chopped dried prunes • chopped Heath bars • chopped malted milk balls • chopped Snickers bars • chopped toasted hazelnuts • chopped walnuts • cocoa nibs • mint chocolate chips • Raisinets • Reese's Pieces • semisweet chocolate chips • white chocolate chips • yellow raisins.

Fat-Free Brownies

Makes sixteen 2¼ × 2¼-inch brownies

You really *can* make a rich brownie that's fat free. These are made with egg whites (save the yolks for another use) and lekvar, a fruit-based fat substitute available in the baking aisle of most supermarkets. To go completely fat-free, ice them with Seven Minute Frosting (page 164) or Vanilla Icing made with fat-free milk (page 166). All the variations keep the recipe fat-free as well!

Nonstick spray for the pan
1 cup all-purpose flour
⅔ cup unsweetened cocoa powder, sifted
1¼ teaspoons baking powder
¼ teaspoon baking soda
¼ teaspoon salt
1 cup sugar
½ cup lekvar (see headnote)
2 teaspoons vanilla extract
3 large egg whites, at room temperature, lightly beaten until frothy
¾ cup plus 1 tablespoon fat-free milk

1. Position the rack in the lower third of the oven. Preheat the oven to 350°F. Oil a 9-inch square baking pan with nonstick spray; set it set aside.

2. In a medium bowl, whisk the flour, cocoa powder, baking powder, baking soda, and salt until well combined. Set aside.

3. In a large bowl, stir the sugar, lekvar, and vanilla with a wooden spoon or a rubber spatula until well combined. Stir in the frothy egg whites just until incorporated. Then stir in the flour mixture in three equal parts, alternating with the milk, as follows: flour, milk, flour, milk, flour. Mix just until the batter is smooth, then spread it gently into the prepared pan.

4. Bake for 25 minutes, or until a toothpick or cake tester comes out with a few moist crumbs attached. The cake should feel springy when touched. Set the pan on a wire rack to cool for at least 1 hour.

5. Cut the brownies into 16 squares while they're still in the pan. Carefully remove them with an offset spatula. Serve immediately, or let cool completely before covering with plastic wrap for storage at room temperature. They will stay fresh for up to 3 days. The brownies can be tightly wrapped in wax paper, sealed in a freezer-safe bag, and frozen for up to 2 months; allow them to thaw at room temperature before serving.

To vary this recipe
Whisk one or more of the following spices into the flour mixture:
2 teaspoons pure chile powder • 1½ teaspoons ground cinnamon • 1 teaspoon ground ginger • ½ teaspoon grated nutmeg

and/or

Substitute one of the following flavorings for the vanilla:

1½ teaspoons banana extract • 1½ teaspoons maple extract • 1½ teaspoons rum extract • 1 teaspoon coconut extract • 1 teaspoon mint extract • 1 teaspoon lemon extract

and/or

Stir in ¾ cup of any of the following mix-ins, or ¾ cup any combination of the following mix-ins, with the flour mixture:

chopped dates • chopped dried apples • chopped dried apricots • chopped dried mango • chopped dried papaya • chopped dried pineapple • chopped dried prunes • dried blueberries • dried cranberries • dried currants • raisins.

Fudge Brownies

Makes sixteen 2 × 2-inch brownies

This is the ultimate fudgy brownie: a chocolate-lover's grail. Basically, there's just enough flour to hold the butter, chocolate, and eggs together. These treats are so dense that they need to cool for 2 hours to set up. They're best unfrosted—but you could throw caution to the wind and ice them with Milk Chocolate Buttercream (page 161). If you do, cut them into very small pieces.

8 tablespoons (1 stick) unsalted butter, plus additional for the pan, at room temperature
9 ounces bittersweet or semisweet chocolate, chopped, or semisweet chocolate chips
2 ounces unsweetened chocolate, chopped
2 large eggs, at room temperature
1 large egg yolk, at room temperature
1 cup sugar
2 teaspoons vanilla extract
⅔ cup all-purpose flour, plus additional for the pan
½ teaspoon salt

1. Position the rack in the lower third of the oven. Preheat the oven to 350°F. Butter and flour an 8-inch square baking pan; set it aside.

2. Place the butter and both kinds of chocolate in the top of a double boiler set over simmering water. If you don't have a double boiler, place the butter and both kinds of chocolate in a heat-safe bowl that fits snugly over a small pot of simmering water. Stir constantly until half the butter and chocolate is melted. Remove the top of the double boiler or the bowl from the pot; then continue stirring, away from the heat, until the butter and chocolate are completely melted. Allow to cool for 10 minutes. (To melt chocolate and butter in a microwave, see pages 9-10.)

3. In a large bowl, beat the eggs, egg yolk, and sugar with a whisk or with an electric mixer at medium speed. Continue beating until the mixture is thick and pale yellow, about 5 minutes by hand or 4 minutes with a mixer. Beat in the vanilla and the chocolate mixture until smooth and uniform.

4. With a wooden spoon or a rubber spatula, stir in the flour and salt just until incorporated. Do not beat. Pour the batter into the prepared pan, spreading it gently to the corners.

5. Bake for 30 minutes. The middle of the cake will be soft; the brownies will set up as they cool. Set the pan on a wire rack to cool for at least 2 hours.

6. Cut the brownies into 16 squares while they're still in the pan. Carefully remove them

with an offset spatula. Serve immediately, or cover with plastic wrap for storage at room temperature. They will stay fresh for up to 5 days. The brownies can also be tightly wrapped in wax paper, sealed in a freezer-safe bag, and frozen for up to 3 months; allow them to thaw at room temperature before serving.

To vary this recipe

Substitute one of the following flavorings for the vanilla:

1½ teaspoons maple extract • 1½ teaspoons rum extract • 1 teaspoon almond extract • 1 teaspoon coconut extract

and/or

Stir in ½ cup of any of the following mix-ins, or ½ cup any combination of the following mix-ins, with the flour mixture:

chopped dried apples • chopped pecans • chopped toasted hazelnuts • chopped unsalted cashews • chopped unsalted roasted peanuts • chopped walnuts • dried blueberries • dried cherries • dried cranberries • raisins • slivered almonds • toasted pepitás.

Gluten-Free Brownies

Makes sixteen 2 × 2-inch brownies

If you have gluten allergies, here's your heaven. These brownies are so tender and chewy, you'll swear there's wheat flour in the batter. Arrowroot flour and xanthum gum are available in many organic markets and in most health-food stores.

8 tablespoons (1 stick) unsalted butter, plus
　additional for the pan, at room temperature
3 ounces unsweetened chocolate, chopped
1 cup sugar
2 large eggs, at room temperature
1 teaspoon gluten-free vanilla extract
¾ cup arrowroot flour
½ teaspoon xanthum gum
½ teaspoon salt

1. Position the rack in the lower third of the oven. Preheat the oven to 350°F. Butter an 8-inch square baking pan; set it aside.

2. Place the butter and chocolate in the top of a double boiler set over simmering water. If you don't have a double boiler, place the butter and chocolate in a heat-safe bowl that fits snugly over a small pot of simmering water. Stir constantly until half the chocolate and butter is melted. Remove the top of the double boiler or the bowl from the pot; then continue stirring, away from the heat, until the chocolate and but-

ter are completely melted. Transfer the mixture to a large bowl and allow to cool for 10 minutes. (To melt chocolate and butter in a microwave, see pages 9-10.)

3. Beat the sugar into the melted chocolate with a whisk or with an electric mixer at medium speed. Continue beating until the mixture is smooth and silky, about 5 minutes by hand or 3 minutes with a mixer. Beat in the eggs and vanilla just until incorporated; then stir in the arrowroot flour, xanthum gum, and salt until smooth, about 2 minutes by hand or 1 minute with a mixer. Spoon the batter into the prepared pan, spreading it gently to the corners.

4. Bake for 25 minutes, or until a toothpick or cake tester comes out clean. Set the pan on a wire rack to cool for at least 30 minutes.

5. Cut the brownies into 16 squares while they're still in the pan. Carefully remove them with an offset spatula. Serve immediately, or let cool completely before covering with plastic wrap for storage at room temperature. They will stay fresh for up to 2 days. The brownies can be tightly wrapped in wax paper, sealed in a freezer-safe bag, and frozen for up to 2 months; allow them to thaw at room temperature before serving.

To vary this recipe

Add one or more of the following spices with the arrowroot flour:

1 teaspoon pure chile powder • ¾ teaspoon ground cinnamon • ½ teaspoon grated nutmeg • ½ teaspoon ground cloves

and/or

Add 1 teaspoon gluten-free maple extract • or 1 teaspoon gluten-free almond extract with the gluten-free vanilla

and/or

Stir in ½ cup of any of the following mix-ins, or ½ cup any combination of the following mix-ins, with the arrowroot flour:

chopped dates • chopped dried prunes • chopped pecans • chopped toasted chickpeas • chopped unsalted roasted peanuts • chopped walnuts • dried cherries • mini marshmallows • unsalted shelled sunflower seeds • yellow raisins.

Honey Brownies

Makes sixteen 2¼ × 2¼-inch brownies

Maison du Chocolat, one of the finest of all chocolatiers, sells a chocolate truffle filled with honey cream. One day, after relishing a few on a walk down Madison Avenue, we thought, why not make brownies with the same flavor? For the best results, use a dark, deeply flavored honey, like pine tree, star thistle, or the so-called Greek honey; or try a rich caramelized honey, such as the Wild West Wildflower sold by Marshall's Farms (see Source Guide).

½ cup all-purpose flour, plus additional for the pan

½ teaspoon baking powder

½ teaspoon salt

9 tablespoons (1 stick plus 1 tablespoon) unsalted butter, plus additional for the pan, at room temperature

2 ounces unsweetened chocolate, chopped

2 ounces bittersweet or semisweet chocolate, chopped, or semisweet chocolate chips

1 cup honey

2 teaspoons vanilla extract

2 large eggs, at room temperature

1. Position the rack in the lower third of the oven. Preheat the oven to 350°F. Butter and flour a 9-inch square baking pan; set it aside.

2. In a medium bowl, whisk the flour, baking powder, and salt until well combined. Set aside.

3. Place the butter and both kinds of chocolate in the top of a double boiler set over simmering water. If you don't have a double boiler, place the butter and both kinds of chocolate in a heat-safe bowl that fits snugly over a small pot of simmering water. Stir constantly until half the butter and chocolate is melted. Remove the top of the double boiler or the bowl from the pot; then continue stirring, away from the heat, until the butter and chocolate are completely melted. Transfer the mixture to a large bowl and allow to cool for 5 minutes. (To melt butter and chocolate in a microwave, see pages 9-10.)

4. Beat the honey and vanilla into the chocolate mixture, using either a wooden spoon or an electric mixer at medium speed. Continue beating until the mixture is smooth, about 4 minutes by hand or 2 minutes with a mixer. Beat in the eggs one at a time, allowing the first to be thoroughly incorporated before adding the second. Scrape down the sides of the bowl as necessary.

5. With a wooden spoon or a rubber spatula, stir in the flour mixture just until incorporated. Do not beat. Pour the batter into the prepared pan, spreading it gently to the corners.

6. Bake for 25 minutes, or until a toothpick or cake tester comes out clean. Set the pan on a wire rack to cool for at least 30 minutes.

7. Cut the brownies into 16 squares while they're still in the pan. Carefully remove them with an offset spatula. Serve immediately, or let cool completely before covering with plastic wrap for storage at room temperature. They will stay fresh for up to 3 days. The brownies can also be tightly wrapped in wax paper, sealed in a freezer-safe bag, and frozen for up to 2 months; allow them to thaw at room temperature before serving.

To vary this recipe
Whisk 1 teaspoon ground ginger or ½ teaspoon grated nutmeg into the flour mixture
and/or
Substitute one of the following flavorings for the vanilla:
1½ teaspoons almond extract • 1½ teaspoons rum extract • 1 teaspoon orange extract

and/or
Stir in ¾ cup of any of the following mix-ins, or ¾ cup any combination of the following mix-ins, with the flour mixture:
almond M & M's • chocolate-covered espresso beans • chopped dried apricots • chopped dried mango • chopped pecans • chopped plain or honey-roasted walnuts • chopped toasted pepitás • chopped unsalted or honey-roasted peanuts • peanut butter chips • pinenuts • semisweet chocolate chips.

Low-Fat Brownies

Makes sixteen 2¼ × 2¼-inch brownies

A low-fat brownie? You don't believe us? OK, you're right—these aren't. They're almost fat-free. The only fat is the cocoa butter in the unsweetened chocolate. As with the Fat-Free Brownies (page 58), lekvar keeps them moist. They're even dense enough to stand up to a thick icing like Seven Minute Frosting (page 164) or Buttercream (page 150). (OK, that last suggestion is a bit like having a cheeseburger with your diet soda—and just as good.)

Vegetable oil spray for the pan
5 ounces unsweetened chocolate, chopped
1¼ cups sugar
½ cup plus 2 tablespoons lekvar
2 teaspoons vanilla extract
4 large egg whites, at room temperature, lightly beaten until frothy
½ cup plus 2 tablespoons all-purpose flour
1¼ teaspoons salt

1. Position the rack in the lower third of the oven. Preheat the oven to 350°F. Oil a 9-inch square baking pan using vegetable oil spray; set it aside.

2. Place the chocolate in the top of a double boiler set over simmering water. If you don't have a double boiler, place the chocolate in a heat-safe bowl that fits snugly over a small pot of simmering water. Stir constantly until half the chocolate is melted. Remove the top of the double boiler or the bowl from the pot; then continue stirring, away from the heat, until the chocolate is completely melted. Allow to cool for 10 minutes. (To melt chocolate in a microwave, see pages 9-10.)

3. In a large bowl, stir the sugar, lekvar, and vanilla together with a wooden spoon or a rubber spatula. Stir in the frothy egg whites just until blended; then stir in the cooled chocolate, working quickly to keep the chocolate from seizing. As soon as the batter is uniform, stir in the flour and salt just until combined. Do not beat. Spoon the batter into the prepared pan, spreading it gently to the corners.

4. Bake for 30 minutes. A toothpick or cake tester may come out damp; the middle should be set but still soft—the brownies will set up as they cool. Set on a wire rack to cool for at least 1 hour.

5. Cut the brownies into 16 squares while they're still in the pan. Carefully remove them with an offset spatula. Serve immediately, or let cool completely before covering with plastic wrap for storage at room temperature. They will stay fresh for up to 2 days. The brownies can be tightly wrapped in wax paper, sealed in a freezer-safe bag, and frozen for up to 1 month; allow them to thaw at room temperature before serving.

To vary this recipe

Stir in one of the following spices with the flour: 1 tablespoon poppy seeds • 1 teaspoon ground cinnamon • 1 teaspoon ground ginger

and/or

Substitute one of the following flavorings for the vanilla:

1½ teaspoons lemon extract • 1½ teaspoons orange extract • 1 teaspoon almond extract

and/or

Stir in ¾ cup of any of the following mix-ins, or ¾ cup any combination of the following mix-ins, with the flour:

chopped dates • chopped dried figs • chopped dried prunes • chopped honey-roasted almonds • chopped honey-roasted peanuts • chopped pistachios • chopped toasted hazelnuts • chopped walnuts • dried cherries • dried currants • shredded sweetened coconut.

Lunchbox Brownies

Makes twenty-four 2¼ × 2⅛-inch brownies

Not so cakey that they go stale, not so fudgy that they make a mess—these are simply the best brownies for lunchboxes, car trips, or picnics. They cut cleanly, wrap up nicely, and freeze well. They're a snap to make and can stand up to almost any mix-in. So what more could anyone want? Oh, they taste great, too.

1½ cups all-purpose flour, plus additional for
   the pan
1 teaspoon baking powder
1 teaspoon salt
½ pound (2 sticks) unsalted butter, plus additional
   for the pan, at room temperature
4 ounces unsweetened chocolate, chopped
2 cups sugar
3 large eggs, at room temperature
1 teaspoon vanilla extract

1. Position the rack in the lower third of the oven. Preheat the oven to 350°F. Butter and flour a 9 × 13-inch baking pan; set it aside.

2. In a medium bowl, whisk the flour, baking powder, and salt until well combined. Set aside.

3. Place the butter and chocolate in the top of a double boiler set over simmering water. If you don't have a double boiler, place the butter and chocolate in a heat-safe bowl that fits snugly over a small pot of simmering water. Stir constantly until half the butter and chocolate is melted. Remove the top of the double boiler or the bowl from the pot; then continue stirring, away from the heat, until the butter and chocolate are completely melted. Transfer the chocolate mixture to a large bowl and allow it to cool for 5 minutes. (To melt butter and chocolate in a microwave, see pages 9-10.)

4. Beat the sugar into the chocolate mixture with a whisk or with an electric mixer at medium speed; continue beating until the mixture is smooth and the sugar is completely dissolved, about 6 minutes by hand or 3 minutes with the mixer. Beat in the eggs one at a time, allowing each to be thoroughly incorporated before adding the next. After beating in the third egg for 1 minute, beat in the vanilla.

5. With a wooden spoon or a rubber spatula, stir in the flour mixture just until incorporated. Do not beat, although the batter will be very thick. Spoon the batter into the prepared pan, spreading it gently to the corners.

6. Bake for 30 minutes, or until a toothpick or cake tester comes out with a few moist crumbs attached. Set the pan on a wire rack and allow to cool for 1 hour.

7. Cut the brownies into 24 pieces while they're still in the pan. Carefully remove them with an offset spatula. Serve immediately, or let cool completely before covering with plastic wrap for storage at room temperature. They will stay fresh for up to 2 days. The brownies can be tightly wrapped in wax paper, sealed in a freezer-safe bag, and frozen for up to 4 months; allow them to thaw at room temperature before serving.

To vary this recipe

Whisk one of the following spices into the flour mixture:

2 teaspoons ground cinnamon • 1 teaspoon ground mace

and/or

Add one of the following flavorings with the vanilla:

2 teaspoons banana extract • 2 teaspoons orange extract • 1½ teaspoons maple extract

and/or

Stir in 1¼ cups of any of the following mix-ins, or 1¼ cups any combination of the following mix-ins, with the flour mixture:

chopped 100 Grand bars • chopped Butterfinger bars • chopped honey-roasted walnuts • chopped KitKat bars • chopped malted milk balls • chopped pecans • chopped toasted hazelnuts • cocoa nibs • crumbled Oreo cookies • dried blueberries • dried cranberries • milk chocolate chips • peanut butter chips • pinenuts • plain or chocolate-covered espresso beans • Raisinets • semisweet chocolate chips • shredded sweetened coconut • toasted pepitás • unsalted shelled sunflower seeds • white chocolate chips.

Malt Brownies

Makes twenty-four 2¼ × 2⅛-inch brownies

Who doesn't like a chocolate malt? So why not make a brownie that tastes like one? These brownies are chewy and thin, fudgy and rich, thick with malt. They're even better the second day, after the malt has infused into the cake.

¾ cup all-purpose flour, plus additional for the pan
1 cup malted milk powder
1 teaspoon baking powder
1 teaspoon salt
½ pound (2 sticks) unsalted butter, plus additional for the pan, at room temperature
4 ounces unsweetened chocolate, chopped
3 ounces semisweet chocolate, chopped, or semisweet chocolate chips
2 cups sugar
3 large eggs, at room temperature
1 teaspoon vanilla extract

1. Position the rack in the lower third of the oven. Preheat the oven to 350°F. Butter and flour a 9 × 13-inch baking pan; set it aside.

2. In a medium bowl, whisk the flour, malted milk powder, baking powder, and salt until well combined. Set aside.

3. Place the butter and both kinds of chocolate in the top of a double boiler set over simmering water. If you don't have a double boiler, place the butter and both kinds of chocolate in a heat-safe bowl that fits snugly over a small pot of simmering water. Stir constantly until half the butter and chocolate is melted. Remove the top of the double boiler or the bowl from the pot; then continue stirring, away from the heat, until the butter and chocolate are completely melted. Transfer the mixture to a large bowl and allow it to cool slightly, about 5 minutes. (To melt butter and chocolate in a microwave, see pages 9-10.)

4. Beat the sugar into the chocolate mixture with a whisk or with an electric mixer at medium speed. Continue beating until the mixture is smooth and uniform, about 6 minutes by hand or 3 minutes with a mixer. Beat in the eggs one at a time, allowing each to be thoroughly incorporated before adding the next. After beating in the third egg for 1 minute, beat in the vanilla.

5. With a wooden spoon or a rubber spatula, stir in the flour mixture just until incorporated. Do not beat. Spoon the batter into the prepared pan, spreading it gently to the corners.

6. Bake for 35 minutes, or until a toothpick or cake tester comes out with a few moist crumbs attached. Set the pan on a wire rack to cool for at least 30 minutes.

7. Cut the brownies into 24 pieces while they're still in the pan. Carefully remove them with an offset spatula. Serve immediately, or let cool completely before covering with plastic wrap for storage at room temperature. They will stay fresh for up to 4 days. The brownies can also be tightly wrapped in wax paper, sealed in a freezer-safe bag, and frozen for up to 3 months; allow them to thaw at room temperature before serving.

To vary this recipe

Stir in 1¼ cups of any of the following mix-ins, or 1¼ cups any combination of the following mix-ins, with the flour mixture:

butterscotch chips • chopped banana chips • chopped malted milk balls • chopped pecans • dried blueberries • dried cherries • dried straw-berries • milk chocolate chips • Reese's Pieces • semisweet chocolate chips • shredded sweetened coconut • slivered almonds • white chocolate chips.

Marble Cheesecake Brownies

Makes sixteen 2¼ × 2¼-inch brownies

If you got a little worried when you saw that the first recipe in this book was Applesauce Brownies, you can put your fears to rest. Here are the most decadent brownies we've ever made: A sweet cream cheese ribbon is swirled into the buttery batter for a treat that's rich, gooey, and still packed with chocolate. Ice them with Chocolate Fudge Frosting (page 152) or—for cream cheese lovers—Cream Cheese Frosting (page 155).

One 8-ounce package cream cheese (regular or low-fat, but not fat-free), softened
1⅓ cups sugar
3 large eggs, at room temperature
2 large egg yolks, at room temperature
1 tablespoon plus 1 teaspoon vanilla extract
12 tablespoons (1½ sticks) unsalted butter, plus additional for the pan, at room temperature
6 ounces bittersweet or semisweet chocolate, chopped, or semisweet chocolate chips
3 ounces unsweetened chocolate, chopped
¾ cup all-purpose flour, plus additional for the pan
½ teaspoon salt

1. In a large bowl, beat the cream cheese and ⅓ cup sugar with an electric mixer at medium speed until the sugar has dissolved and the mixture is smooth, about 4 minutes, scraping down the sides of the bowl as necessary. Beat in 1 egg

and 1 teaspoon vanilla until well combined. Set aside.

2. Position the rack in the lower third of the oven. Preheat the oven to 350°F. Butter and flour a 9-inch square baking pan; set it aside.

3. Place the butter and both kinds of chocolate in the top of a double boiler set over simmering water. If you don't have a double boiler, place the butter and both kinds of chocolate in a heat-safe bowl that fits snugly over a small pot of simmering water. Stir constantly until half the butter and chocolate is melted. Remove the top of the double boiler or the bowl from the pot; then continue stirring, away from the heat, until the butter and chocolate are completely melted. Transfer the mixture to a large bowl and allow to cool for 10 minutes. (To melt butter and chocolate in a microwave, see pages 9-10.)

4. Beat the remaining 1 cup sugar into the melted chocolate with a whisk or with an electric mixer at medium speed; continue beating until the mixture is smooth and silky, about 5 minutes by hand or 2 minutes with a mixer. Beat in the remaining 2 eggs, 2 egg yolks, and 1 tablespoon vanilla until incorporated.

5. With a wooden spoon or a rubber spatula, stir in the flour and salt just until combined. Do not beat. Spread three-quarters of this chocolate batter into the prepared pan. Cover with the cream cheese mixture, spreading it as evenly as possible with a spatula. Do not press down. Dot the cream cheese mixture with the remaining chocolate batter, using heaping tablespoons of batter.

6. To create a swirl effect in the brownies, run a sharp kitchen knife through the batter without touching the bottom of the pan or lifting the knife up during its course. Slice through the chocolate dollops and drag some of the mixture into the cream cheese. Continue swirling until a spun-out, almost psychedelic pattern has formed.

7. Bake for 35 minutes, or until a toothpick or cake tester comes out clean. Set the pan on a wire rack to cool for at least 30 minutes.

8. Cut the brownies into 16 squares while they're still in the pan. Carefully remove them with an offset spatula. Serve immediately, or let cool completely before covering with plastic wrap for storage at room temperature. They will stay fresh for up to 4 days. The brownies can be tightly wrapped in wax paper, sealed in a freezer-safe bag, and frozen for up to 3 months; allow them to thaw at room temperature before serving.

To vary this recipe
Substitute one of the following flavorings for the 1 tablespoon vanilla used in the chocolate batter: 2½ teaspoons almond extract • 2½ teaspoons maple extract • 2 teaspoons banana extract • 2 teaspoons coconut extract • 2 teaspoons mint extract • 2 teaspoons rum extract
and/or
Stir in ¾ cup of any of the following mix-ins, or ¾ cup any combination of the following mix-ins, with the flour mixture in the chocolate batter:
chopped candied chestnuts • chopped candied orange peel • chopped Heath bars • chopped Oh Henry! bars • chopped pecans • chopped walnuts • cocoa nibs • dried cherries • shredded sweetened coconut • white chocolate chips.

Marmalade Brownies

Makes sixteen 2¼ × 2¼-inch brownies

The French confections called *orang-ettes* are made of candied orange rind enrobed in dark chocolate. They're our favorite Parisian treat, perfect for strolling the rue Saint Honoré. The easiest way to replicate that taste in a brownie is with a strong, dense, chunky, and slightly sour marmalade—any of the British varieties sold in gourmet markets and specialty stores will do the trick. Great on their own, these brownies can also be iced with Ganache Icing (page 157) or even Sour Cream Icing (page 165).

¾ cup plus 1 tablespoon all-purpose flour, plus additional for the pan

½ teaspoon baking soda

½ teaspoon salt

10 tablespoons (1 stick plus 2 tablespoons) unsalted butter, plus additional for the pan, at room temperature

3 ounces bittersweet or semisweet chocolate, chopped, or semisweet chocolate chips

2 ounces unsweetened chocolate, chopped

¾ cup sugar

½ cup orange marmalade

2 large eggs, at room temperature

1 teaspoon vanilla extract

1 teaspoon grated orange zest (optional)

1. Position the rack in the lower third of the oven. Preheat the oven to 350°F. Butter and flour a 9-inch square baking pan; set it aside.

2. In a medium bowl, whisk the flour, baking powder, and salt until well combined. Set aside.

3. Place the butter and both kinds of chocolate in the top of a double boiler set over simmering water. If you don't have a double boiler, place the butter and both kinds of chocolate in a heat-safe bowl that fits snugly over a small pot of simmering water. Stir constantly until half the butter and chocolate is melted. Remove the top of the double boiler or the bowl from the pot; then continue stirring, away from the heat, until the butter and chocolate are completely melted. Allow to cool for 10 minutes. (To melt butter and chocolate in a microwave, see pages 9-10.)

4. In a large bowl, beat the sugar, marmalade, and eggs with an electric mixer at medium speed. Continue beating for 4 minutes, until the mixture is smooth and uniform, scraping down the sides of the bowl as necessary. Beat in the cooled chocolate mixture, vanilla, and orange zest, if desired, until smooth, about 2 minutes.

5. With a wooden spoon or a rubber spatula, stir in the flour mixture just until incorporated. Do not beat. Pour the batter into the prepared pan, spreading it gently to the corners.

6. Bake for 20 minutes, or until a toothpick or cake tester comes out clean. Set the pan on a wire rack to cool for at least 1 hour.

7. Cut the brownies into 16 squares while they're still in the pan. Carefully remove them with an offset spatula. Serve immediately, or let cool completely before covering with plastic wrap for storage at room temperature. They will stay fresh for up to 4 days. Because of the additional moisture in the marmalade, these brownies do not freeze well.

To vary this recipe
Omit the orange zest and substitute any of the following for the orange marmalade:
apricot jam • blueberry preserves • ginger conserve • grape jam • peach jam • pear preserves • prepared mincemeat • sour cherry preserves • strawberry preserves

and/or
Stir in ¾ cup of any of the following mix-ins, or ¾ cup any combination of the following mix-ins, with the flour mixture:
chopped candied chestnuts • chopped toasted hazelnuts • chopped walnuts • mini marshmallows • semisweet chocolate chips • shredded sweetened coconut.

Marshmallow Brownies

Makes twenty-four 2¼ × 2⅛-inch brownies

Sticky Marshmallow Fluff causes these chewy brownies to collapse while baking—they become gooey, rich treats, sure to please. Try crumbling some into homemade vanilla ice cream during its last few turns in the ice cream maker, or serving them with chocolate or vanilla pudding.

¾ cup all-purpose flour, plus additional for the pan

½ teaspoon baking powder

½ teaspoon salt

12 tablespoons (1½ sticks) unsalted butter, plus additional for the pan, at room temperature

4 ounces bittersweet or semisweet chocolate, chopped, or semisweet chocolate chips

2 ounces unsweetened chocolate, chopped

1½ cups sugar

2 large eggs, at room temperature

1 teaspoon vanilla extract

One 7½-ounce jar Marshmallow Fluff or other marshmallow creme

1. Position the rack in the lower third of the oven. Preheat the oven to 350°F. Butter and flour a 9 × 13-inch baking pan; set it aside.

2. In a medium bowl, whisk the flour, baking powder, and salt until well combined. Set aside.

3. Place 4 tablespoons (½ stick) butter and both kinds of chocolate in the top of a double boiler set over simmering water. If you don't have a double boiler, place 4 tablespoons butter and both kinds of chocolate in a heat-safe bowl that fits snugly over a small pot of simmering water. Stir constantly until half the butter and chocolate is melted. Remove the top of the double boiler or the bowl from the pot; then continue stirring, away from heat, until the butter and chocolate are completely melted. Allow to cool for 10 minutes. (To melt butter and chocolate in a microwave, see pages 9-10.)

4. In a large bowl, cream the remaining 8 tablespoons (1 stick) butter and sugar with an electric mixer at medium speed; continue beating until the mixture is pale yellow and thick, about 5 minutes. Beat in the eggs one at a time, allowing the first to be thoroughly incorporated before adding the second. After beating in the second egg for 1 minute, add the vanilla, then the Marshmallow Fluff. Beat at medium-high speed until the mixture is smooth and uniform, about 3 minutes, scraping down the sides of the bowl as necessary.

5. With the mixer at low speed, stir in the flour mixture just until incorporated. Do not overmix, although the batter will be quite stiff.

Spoon the batter into the prepared pan, spreading it gently to the corners.

6. Bake for 27 minutes. The cake should be soft at the center. Set the pan on a wire rack to cool for at least 2 hours.

7. Cut the brownies into 24 pieces while they're still in the pan. Carefully remove them with an offset spatula. Serve immediately, or cover with plastic wrap for storage at room temperature. They will stay fresh for up to 4 days. Because of the Marshmallow Fluff, these brownies do not freeze well.

To vary this recipe
Reduce the flour to ½ cup and add ¼ cup finely ground almonds
or
Stir in 1 cup of any of the following mix-ins, or 1 cup any combination of the following mix-ins, with the flour mixture:
chopped pecans • chopped toasted hazelnuts • chopped walnuts • cocoa nibs • dried cranberries • dried currants • peanut butter chips • raisins • semisweet chocolate chips • slivered almonds • white chocolate chips.

Marzipan Brownies

Makes sixteen 2 × 2-inch brownies

Flavored with marzipan, or almond paste, these brownies are reminiscent of the small chocolate cakes that are popular during the holidays in the Frisian areas of the Netherlands. You'll need a food processor to turn the paste into a batter. You can also use an electric mixer at medium speed, but only if the marzipan is fresh and quite soft.

⅓ cup all-purpose flour, plus additional for the pan
½ teaspoon baking soda
½ teaspoon salt
8 tablespoons (1 stick) unsalted butter, plus additional for the pan, at room temperature
3 ounces unsweetened chocolate, chopped
One 7-ounce tube marzipan or almond paste
½ cup sugar
2 large eggs, at room temperature
½ teaspoon almond extract (optional)

1. Position the rack in the lower third of the oven. Preheat the oven to 350°F. Butter and flour an 8-inch square baking pan; set it aside.

2. In a medium bowl, whisk the flour, baking soda, and salt until well combined. Set aside.

3. Place the butter and chocolate in the top of a double boiler set over simmering water. If you don't have a double boiler, place the chocolate and butter in a heat-safe bowl that fits snugly over a small pot of simmering water. Stir constantly until half the butter and chocolate is melted. Remove the top of the double boiler or the bowl from the pot; then continue stirring, away from the heat, until the butter and chocolate are completely melted. Allow to cool for 5 minutes. (To melt butter and chocolate in a microwave, see pages 9-10).

4. Process the marzipan and sugar in a food processor until the mixture is thick and uniform. Add the eggs, and process until the mixture is uniform, about 1 minute. With the machine running, pour the cooled chocolate mixture through the feed tube. Scrape down the sides of the bowl and the central blade mechanism as necessary. Process for 2 minutes, then remove the cover to add the dry ingredients and the almond extract, if desired. Cover and process until the batter is smooth, about 2 minutes. Spread the batter into the prepared pan; since it is very thick, use a spatula or wooden spoon to smooth it to the corners.

5. Bake for 22 minutes, or until a toothpick or cake tester comes out with a few moist crumbs attached. Set the pan on a wire rack to cool for at least 30 minutes.

6. Cut the brownies into 16 squares while they're still in the pan. Carefully remove them with an offset spatula. Serve immediately, or let cool completely before covering with plastic wrap for storage at room temperature. They will stay fresh for up to 4 days. The brownies can also be tightly wrapped in wax paper, sealed in a freezer-safe bag, and frozen for up to 3 months; allow them to thaw at room temperature before serving.

To vary this recipe

Whisk one of the following flavorings into the flour mixture:

1 teaspoon finely grated orange zest • 1 teaspoon ground ginger • ½ teaspoon ground cloves • ½ teaspoon ground mace

and/or

Stir in ½ cup of any of the following mix-ins, or ½ cup any combination of the following mix-ins, with the flour mixture:

chopped banana chips • chopped pecans • chopped toasted hazelnuts • cocoa nibs • dried blueberries • dried cherries • dried currants • milk chocolate chips • Reese's Pieces • semi-sweet chocolate chips • toasted pepitás • white chocolate chips.

Mayonnaise Brownies

Makes sixteen 2¼ × 2¼-inch brownies

Chocolate mayonnaise cakes were once a staple in the South. Since mayonnaise is little more than eggs and oil, the cake turns out naturally dense and quite fudgy. We couldn't resist turning that old classic into a thick, gooey brownie. If you want, ice these with Cocoa Frosting (page 153), Chocolate Drizzle (page 151), or an old-time Southern favorite, Cola Icing (page 154).

Unsalted butter for the pan
½ cup unsweetened cocoa powder, sifted
½ cup boiling water
1 tablespoon vanilla extract
1½ cups all-purpose flour, plus additional for the pan
1½ cups sugar
½ teaspoon baking powder
¼ teaspoon baking soda
¼ teaspoon salt
½ cup mayonnaise (regular or low-fat, but not fat-free)
2 large eggs, at room temperature

1. Position the rack in the lower third of the oven. Preheat the oven to 350°F. Butter and flour a 9-inch square baking pan; set it aside.

2. In a small bowl, whisk the cocoa powder, boiling water, and vanilla until smooth, like hot cocoa. Set aside.

3. In a large bowl, whisk the flour, sugar, baking powder, baking soda, and salt until well combined. Beat the cocoa mixture into the dry ingredients with an electric mixer at low speed for 1 minute, then at high speed for 3 minutes, until the sugar has dissolved and the mixture is smooth. Scrape down the sides of the bowl as necessary. Add the mayonnaise and eggs all at once; beat at medium speed for 2 minutes, until uniform. Pour the batter into the prepared pan, spreading it gently to the corners.

4. Bake for 35 minutes, or until a toothpick or cake tester comes out with many moist crumbs attached. The center of the cake will be soft. Set the pan on a wire rack to cool for at least 2 hours.

5. Cut the brownies into 16 squares while they're still in the pan. Carefully remove them with an offset spatula. Serve immediately, or cover with plastic wrap for storage at room temperature. They will stay fresh for up to 3 days. Because of the mayonnaise, these brownies do not freeze well.

To vary this recipe
Add one of the following with the vanilla:
1 tablespoon diced crystallized ginger • 1 teaspoon lemon extract • 1 teaspoon rum extract *and/or*

Stir in ¾ cup of any of the following mix-ins, or ¾ cup any combination of the following mix-ins, after beating in the eggs:

chopped dried figs • chopped dried mango • chopped dried papaya • chopped pecans • chopped walnuts • cocoa nibs • crumbled biscotti • crumbled gingersnap cookies • crumbled molasses cookies.

Mexican Chocolate Brownies

Makes twenty-four 2¼ × 2⅛-inch brownies

Mexican chocolate is actually a combination of chocolate, ground cocoa nibs, and cinnamon. Although most people use it for hot chocolate, it's even better in brownies. The best-known brand, Ibarra, comes in 3¼-ounce rounds; other varieties can also include ground almonds and/or ground cloves. Any will work in this recipe, although the additional flavorings in some will make the final brownies spicier. Ice them with a dense icing such as Marshmallow Cream Frosting (page 160) or Peanut Butter Icing (page 163).

1¾ cups all-purpose flour, plus additional for the pan

½ teaspoon baking powder

½ teaspoon salt

12 tablespoons (1½ sticks) unsalted butter, plus additional for the pan, at room temperature

9¾ ounces Mexican chocolate, such as 3 rounds of Ibarra, chopped

2 ounces unsweetened chocolate, chopped

1 cup plus 2 tablespoons packed light brown sugar

3 large eggs, at room temperature

2 teaspoons vanilla extract

1. Position the rack in the lower third of the oven. Preheat the oven to 350°F. Butter and flour a 9 × 13-inch baking pan; set it aside.

2. In a medium bowl, whisk the flour, baking powder, and salt until well combined. Set aside.

3. Place the butter and both kinds of chocolate in the top of a double boiler set over simmering water. If you don't have a double boiler, place the butter and both kinds of chocolate in a heat-safe bowl that fits snugly over a small pot of simmering water. Stir constantly until half the butter and chocolate is melted. Remove the top of the double boiler or the bowl from the pot; then continue stirring, away from the heat, until the butter and chocolate are completely melted. Transfer the mixture to a large bowl and allow to cool for 10 minutes. (To melt butter and chocolate in a microwave, see pages 9-10.)

4. Beat the brown sugar into the melted chocolate with a whisk or with an electric mixer at medium speed; continue beating until the mixture is smooth and silky, about 7 minutes by hand or 4 minutes with a mixer. Beat in the eggs one at a time, allowing each to be thoroughly incorporated before adding the next. After beating in the third egg for 1 minute, stir in the vanilla.

5. With a wooden spoon or a rubber spatula, stir in the flour mixture just until combined. Do not beat. Spoon the batter into the prepared pan, spreading it gently to the corners.

6. Bake for 25 minutes, or until a toothpick or cake tester comes out with a few moist crumbs attached. Set the pan on a wire rack to cool for at least 30 minutes.

7. Cut the brownies into 24 pieces while they're still in the pan. Carefully remove them with an offset spatula. Serve immediately, or let cool completely before covering with plastic wrap for storage at room temperature. They will stay fresh for up to 4 days. The brownies can be tightly wrapped in wax paper, sealed in a freezer-safe bag, and frozen for up to 4 months; allow them to thaw at room temperature before serving.

To vary this recipe

Whisk 2 teaspoons pure chile powder into the flour mixture

and/or

Add 1 teaspoon almond extract with the vanilla

and/or

Stir in ¾ cup of the following mix-ins, or ¾ cup any combination of the following mix-ins, with the flour mixture:

chopped dried papaya • chopped dried prunes • chopped honey-roasted peanuts • chopped pecans • milk chocolate chips • mini marshmallows • plain or chocolate-covered espresso beans • raisins • shredded sweetened coconut • toasted pepitás • white chocolate chips.

Milk Chocolate Brownies

Makes sixteen 2¼ × 2¼-inch brownies

Because of the additional dairy fat in milk chocolate, these brownies resemble a cross between milk chocolate fudge and rich underbaked chocolate custard cakes. As the recipe indicates, they come out of the oven slightly underbaked and then stand for 2 hours to allow the chocolate to set up.

¾ cup all-purpose flour, plus additional for the pan
½ teaspoon baking powder
½ teaspoon salt
1 pound milk chocolate, chopped, or milk chocolate chips
8 tablespoons (1 stick) unsalted butter, cut into 1-tablespoon chunks, plus additional for the pan, at room temperature
¾ cup sugar
3 large eggs, at room temperature

1. Position the rack in the lower third of the oven. Preheat the oven to 350°F. Butter and flour a 9-inch square baking pan; set it aside.

2. In a medium bowl, whisk the flour, baking powder, and salt until well combined. Set aside.

3. Place the milk chocolate in the top of a double boiler set over simmering water. If you don't have a double boiler, place the milk chocolate in a heat-safe bowl that fits snugly over a small pot of simmering water. Stir constantly until the chocolate is almost completely melted. Remove the top of the double boiler or the bowl from the pot. Stir in the butter, one piece at a time, away from the heat, until the chocolate is completely melted and all the butter is incorporated. (To melt chocolate in a microwave, see pages 9-10.)

4. In a large mixing bowl, beat the sugar and eggs with an electric mixer at medium speed until the mixture is pale yellow and thick, about 4 minutes. With the mixer running, slowly pour in the chocolate mixture. Scrape down the sides of the bowl as necessary. Continue beating at medium speed until the mixture is smooth and silky, about 5 minutes.

5. With a wooden spoon or a rubber spatula, stir in the flour mixture just until combined. Do not beat. Spoon the batter into the prepared pan, spreading it gently to the corners.

6. Bake for 25 minutes. The cake will be soft in the middle—it will firm as it cools. Set the pan on a wire rack to cool for at least 2 hours.

7. Cut the brownies into 16 squares while they're still in the pan. Carefully remove them with an offset spatula. Serve immediately, or cover with plastic wrap for storage at room temperature. They will stay fresh for up to 2 days.

The brownies can be tightly wrapped in wax paper, sealed in a freezer-safe bag, and frozen for up to 2 months; allow them to thaw at room temperature before serving.

To vary this recipe

Whisk one or more of the following spices into the flour mixture:

2 teaspoons ground cinnamon • 2 teaspoons ground ginger • 1 teaspoon grated nutmeg • ¾ teaspoon mace • ½ teaspoon ground cloves

and/or

Stir in ¾ cup of any of the following mix-ins, or ¾ cup any combination of the following mix-ins, with the flour mixture:

chopped banana chips • chopped caramels • chopped Heath bars • chopped honey-roasted peanuts • chopped Snickers bars • chopped toasted hazelnuts • chopped unsalted cashews • chopped walnuts • cocoa nibs • mint chocolate chips • peanut butter chips • raspberry chocolate chips.

Mint Brownies

Makes twenty-four $2\frac{1}{4} \times 2\frac{1}{8}$-inch brownies

With its chocolate cookie crust and rich crème de menthe filling, grasshopper pie was once a summertime favorite. In this brownie version, we use peppermint extract because crème de menthe adds too much moisture to the batter. Peppermint extract is available in the baking aisle of most supermarkets and gourmet stores. Top these with Grasshopper Frosting (page 158).

1¼ cups all-purpose flour, plus additional for the pan
1 teaspoon salt
½ teaspoon baking powder
½ teaspoon baking soda
12 tablespoons (1½ sticks) unsalted butter, plus additional for the pan, at room temperature
6 ounces unsweetened chocolate, chopped
4 ounces bittersweet or semisweet chocolate, chopped, or semisweet chocolate chips
1¾ cups sugar
4 large eggs, at room temperature
½ teaspoon vanilla extract
½ teaspoon peppermint extract

1. Position the rack in the lower third of the oven. Preheat the oven to 350°F. Butter and flour a 9×13-inch baking pan; set it aside.

2. In a medium bowl, whisk the flour, salt, baking powder, and baking soda until well combined. Set aside.

3. Place the butter and both kinds of chocolate in the top of a double boiler set over simmering water. If you don't have a double boiler, place the butter and both kinds of chocolate in a heat-safe bowl that fits snugly over a small pot of simmering water. Stir constantly until half the butter and chocolate is melted. Remove the top of the double boiler or the bowl from the pot; then continue stirring, away from the heat, until the butter and chocolate are completely melted. Transfer the mixture to a large bowl and allow to cool for 5 minutes. (To melt butter and chocolate in a microwave, see pages 9-10.)

4. Beat the sugar into the melted chocolate mixture with a whisk or with an electric mixer at medium speed; continue beating until the mixture is smooth and silky, about 5 minutes by hand or 3 minutes with a mixer. Beat in the eggs one at a time, allowing each to be thoroughly incorporated before adding the next. After beating in the fourth egg for 1 minute, add the vanilla and peppermint extracts.

5. With a wooden spoon or a rubber spatula, stir in the flour mixture just until combined. Do not beat. Pour the batter into the prepared pan, spreading it gently to the corners.

6. Bake for 30 minutes, or until a toothpick or cake tester comes out with a few moist crumbs attached. Set the pan on a wire rack to cool for at least 1 hour.

7. Cut the brownies into 24 pieces while they're still in the pan. Carefully remove them with an offset spatula. Serve immediately, or let cool completely before covering with plastic wrap for storage at room temperature. They will stay fresh for up to 2 days. The brownies can be tightly wrapped in wax paper, sealed in a freezer-safe bag, and frozen for up to 2 months; allow them to thaw at room temperature before serving.

To vary this recipe

Stir in 1¼ cups of any of the following mix-ins, or 1¼ cups any combination of the following mix-ins, with the flour mixture:

chopped Baby Ruth bars • chopped dried apples • chopped dried mango • cocoa nibs • dried cherries • dried currants • Goobers • milk chocolate chips • mini marshmallows • mint chocolate chips • Raisinets • raspberry chocolate chips • semisweet chocolate chips • white chocolate chips.

Oat Brownies

Makes sixteen $2\frac{1}{4} \times 2\frac{1}{4}$-inch brownies

These brownies have a hearty but sweet crunch, like chocolate-covered granola. Use rolled oats, not quick-cooking, and toast them on a cookie sheet in a 350°F oven for 5 to 7 minutes, tossing once or twice. The brownies will stand up to any frosting, but they are also good sprinkled with chopped walnuts and drizzled with honey.

½ cup all-purpose flour, plus additional for the pan
½ teaspoon baking powder
½ teaspoon salt
8 tablespoons (1 stick) unsalted butter, plus additional for the pan
2 ounces bittersweet or semisweet chocolate, chopped, or semisweet chocolate chips
2 ounces unsweetened chocolate, chopped
1 cup packed light brown sugar
½ cup granulated sugar
2 large eggs, at room temperature
2 teaspoons vanilla extract
1½ cups rolled oats (not quick-cooking), toasted (see headnote)

1. Position the rack in the lower third of the oven. Preheat the oven to 350°F. Butter and flour a 9-inch square baking pan; set it aside.

2. In a medium bowl, whisk the flour, baking powder, and salt until well combined. Set aside.

3. Place the butter and both kinds of chocolate in the top of a double boiler set over simmering water. If you don't have a double boiler, place the butter and both kinds of chocolate in a heat-safe bowl that fits snugly over a small pot of simmering water. Stir constantly until half the butter and chocolate is melted. Remove the top of the double boiler or the bowl from the pot; then continue stirring, away from the heat, until the butter and chocolate are completely melted. Allow to cool for 10 minutes. (To melt butter and chocolate in a microwave, see pages 9-10.)

4. In a large bowl, beat the brown sugar, granulated sugar, and eggs with a whisk or with an electric mixer at medium speed. Continue beating until the sugar has dissolved and the mixture is thick and creamy, about 6 minutes by hand or 3 minutes with a mixer. Beat in the vanilla, then the cooled chocolate mixture; continue beating until smooth and uniform, about 2 minutes, scraping down the sides of the bowl as necessary.

5. With a wooden spoon or a rubber spatula, stir in the rolled oats, then the flour mixture, just until incorporated. Do not beat. Spoon the batter into the prepared pan, spreading it gently to the corners.

6. Bake for 20 minutes, or until a toothpick or cake tester comes out with a few moist crumbs attached. Set the pan on a wire rack to cool for at least 30 minutes.

7. Cut the brownies into 16 squares while they're still in the pan. Carefully remove them with an offset spatula. Serve immediately, or let cool completely before covering with plastic wrap for storage at room temperature. They will stay fresh for 2 days. The brownies may also be wrapped tightly in wax paper, sealed in a freezer-safe bag, and frozen for up to 1 month; allow them to thaw at room temperature before serving.

To vary this recipe
Whisk one or more of the following spices into the flour mixture:
2 teaspoons ground cinnamon • 1½ teaspoons ground ginger • ½ teaspoon grated nutmeg

and/or
Add 2 teaspoons maple extract • or 2 teaspoons rum extract with the vanilla
and/or
Stir in ¾ cup of any of the following mix-ins, or ¾ cup any combination of the following mix-ins, with the rolled oats:
chopped dried papaya • chopped Heath bars • chopped honey-roasted almonds • chopped toasted hazelnuts • crumbled biscotti • crumbled molasses cookies • dried cranberries • granola • mini marshmallows • raisins • Reese's Pieces • shredded sweetened coconut • unsalted shelled sunflower seeds.

Passover Brownies

Makes sixteen 2¼ × 2¼-inch brownies

These fudgy brownies don't fake it. Some Passover recipes make substitutions for the missing flour, as if tricking you into forgetting it's missing. But these are made with ground almonds, so they're more like a flourless chocolate cake, rich and moist. As a bonus, there's no butter in the batter, so they can even be eaten after a meat meal. We think you should try them anytime of the year for an intensely chocolate treat.

Vegetable oil or margarine for the pan
1 cup sugar
¼ cup vegetable oil
3 large eggs, separated, at room temperature
½ teaspoon vanilla extract
½ teaspoon salt
½ cup unsweetened cocoa powder, sifted, plus additional for the pan
½ cup finely ground almonds
2 large egg whites, at room temperature

1. Position the rack in the lower third of the oven. Preheat the oven to 350°F. Grease a 9-inch square baking pan, using vegetable oil or margarine. Dust the pan with cocoa powder and set it aside.

2. In a large bowl, beat the sugar and oil with an electric mixer at medium speed until well com-bined. Add the 3 egg yolks all at once, and beat until thoroughly incorporated. Then add the vanilla and salt, scraping down the sides of the bowl as necessary. Once the mixture is uniform, beat in the cocoa powder and ground almonds at low speed. The mixture will be very thick.

3. Having cleaned and dried the mixer beaters, whip all the egg whites until frothy in a separate large bowl with the mixer at medium speed; increase the speed to high and beat until soft peaks form, about 3 minutes.

4. Beat half the beaten egg whites into the choco-late mixture to soften it, using the mixer at low speed. Gently fold the remaining egg whites into the chocolate mixture with a rubber spatula or a wooden spoon. Stir just until incorporated; do not beat. Gently spread the batter into the prepared pan, taking care not to break up the air bubbles.

5. Bake for 20 minutes, or until the cake is soft but set; a toothpick or cake tester should come out with wet crumbs attached. Set the pan on a wire rack to cool for at least 2 hours.

6. Cut the brownies into 16 squares while they're still in the pan. Carefully remove them with an offset spatula. Serve immediately, or cover with plastic wrap for storage at room temperature. They will stay fresh for up to 3 days. The brownies can be tightly wrapped in wax paper, sealed in a freezer-safe bag, and frozen for up to 2 months; allow them to thaw at room temperature before serving.

To vary this recipe
Add one or more of the following spices with the vanilla:

1½ teaspoons ground cinnamon • 1 teaspoon ground ginger • 1 teaspoon ground mace • ½ teaspoon grated nutmeg

and/or
Stir in ¾ cup of any of the following mix-ins, or ¾ cup any combination of the following mix-ins, with the egg whites:

chopped almonds • chopped dates • chopped dried figs • chopped dried pineapple • chopped dried prunes • chopped walnuts • dried cherries • raisins • semisweet chocolate chips • unsalted shelled sunflower seeds • white chocolate chips.

Peanut Butter Brownies

Makes twenty-four $2\frac{1}{4} \times 2\frac{1}{8}$-inch brownies

Like a good peanut butter cup, these brownies are diet-busters, and worth every bite. If you don't want your brownies quite so fudgy—although with this much chocolate, butter, and peanut butter, it's rather hard to get around it—omit rapping the baking pan on the oven shelf during baking. These brownies are also good right out of the freezer, like frozen candy bars.

1 cup all-purpose flour, plus additional for the pan

½ teaspoon salt

¼ teaspoon baking soda

12 tablespoons (1½ sticks) unsalted butter, plus additional for the pan, at room temperature

9 ounces bittersweet or semisweet chocolate, chopped, or semisweet chocolate chips

3 ounces unsweetened chocolate, chopped

1 cup granulated sugar

½ cup packed dark brown sugar

2 large eggs, at room temperature

2 large egg yolks, at room temperature

1 cup creamy peanut butter

2 teaspoons vanilla extract

1. Position the rack in the lower third of the oven. Preheat the oven to 350°F. Butter and flour a 9×13-inch baking pan; set it aside.

2. In a medium bowl, whisk the flour, salt, and baking soda until well combined. Set aside.

3. Place 6 tablespoons butter and both kinds of chocolate in the top of a double boiler set over simmering water. If you don't have a double boiler, place 6 tablespoons butter and both kinds of chocolate in a heat-safe bowl that fits snugly over a small pot of simmering water. Stir constantly until half the butter and chocolate is melted. Remove the top of the double boiler or the bowl from the pot; then continue stirring, away from the heat, until the butter and chocolate are completely melted. Allow to cool for 10 minutes. (To melt butter and chocolate in a microwave, see pages 9-10.)

4. Place the granulated sugar and the brown sugar in a large bowl. Beat in one egg at a time, using an electric mixer at medium speed. Once the mixture is smooth, beat in both egg yolks at once. Continue beating at medium speed until pale brown and light, about 3 minutes. Beat in the remaining 6 tablespoons butter, 1 tablespoon at a time. Continue beating until the mixture is creamy, about 5 minutes. Then beat in the peanut butter, vanilla, and cooled chocolate mixture until smooth, about 2 minutes, scraping down the sides of the bowl as necessary.

5. With a wooden spoon or a rubber spatula, stir in the flour mixture just until incorporated. Do not beat, although the batter will be very thick. Spoon the batter into the prepared pan, spreading it gently to the corners.

6. Bake for 15 minutes, then rap the pan three or four times on the oven rack. Bake for an additional 12 minutes, or until a toothpick or cake tester comes out with a few moist crumbs attached. Set the pan on a wire rack to cool for at least 30 minutes.

7. Cut the brownies into 24 pieces while they're still in the pan. Carefully remove them with an offset spatula. Serve immediately, or let cool completely before covering with plastic wrap for storage at room temperature. They will stay fresh for up to 4 days. The brownies can also be tightly wrapped in wax paper, sealed in a freezer-safe bag, and frozen for up to 3 months; allow them to thaw at room temperature before serving.

To vary this recipe
Add 1½ teaspoons maple extract • or 1 teaspoon banana extract with the vanilla.
and/or
Stir in 1¼ cups of any of the following mix-ins, or 1¼ cups any combination of the following mix-ins, with the flour mixture:
chopped honey-roasted peanuts • chopped peanut brittle • chopped pecans • chopped toasted chickpeas • chopped walnuts • Goobers • peanut M & M's • Raisinets • raisins • semisweet chocolate chips • white chocolate chips.

Pear Brownies

Makes twenty-four 2¼ × 2⅛-inch brownies

A coffee-cake/brownie hybrid, this brownie tastes best if the pears are very ripe. To ripen them, seal them in a paper bag and set them out on the counter overnight, or for up to 48 hours, checking them occasionally. Use them when they have a few brown spots and the flesh is soft and juicy.

4 ripe Bartlett pears
1 cup sugar
Unsalted butter for the pan
2 large eggs, at room temperature
⅔ cup canola oil
1 teaspoon vanilla extract
¾ cup all-purpose flour, plus additional for the pan
½ cup unsweetened cocoa powder, sifted
1 teaspoon baking powder
1 teaspoon baking soda
1 teaspoon salt

1. Peel and core the pears. Cut them into 1-inch cubes. Toss the pieces in a medium bowl with the sugar; set aside for 15 minutes to let the pears macerate.

2. Position the rack in the lower third of the oven. Preheat the oven to 350°F. Butter and flour a 9 × 13-inch baking pan; set it aside.

3. In a medium bowl, whisk the eggs, oil, and vanilla until well combined. Add the pear mixture and stir until the pieces are coated.

4. In a large bowl, whisk the flour, cocoa powder, baking powder, baking soda, and salt until well combined. Stir in the pear mixture with a wooden spoon; stir until moistened, but do not beat. Pour the batter into the prepared pan, spreading it gently to the corners.

5. Bake for 30 minutes, or until a toothpick or cake tester comes out with a few moist crumbs attached. Set the pan on a wire rack to cool for at least 1 hour.

6. Cut the brownies into 24 pieces while they're still in the pan. Carefully remove them with an offset spatula. Serve immediately, or let cool completely before covering with plastic wrap for storage at room temperature. They will stay fresh for up to 4 days. These brownies do not freeze well because the pear chunks get too icy.

To vary this recipe
Whisk one or more of the following spices into the flour mixture:
2 tablespoons poppy seeds • 2 teaspoons ground cinnamon • 1½ teaspoons ground ginger • 1 teaspoon ground mace • ½ teaspoon grated nutmeg
and/or
Add 1 teaspoon maple extract • or 1 teaspoon rum extract with the vanilla

and/or

Stir in 1¼ cups of any of the following mix-ins, or 1¼ cups any combination of the following mix-ins, with the flour mixture:

almond M & M's • chopped caramels • chopped toasted hazelnuts • chopped walnuts • cocoa nibs • crumbled biscotti • crumbled gingersnap cookies • dried cherries • dried cranberries • dried currants • peanut butter chips • semisweet chocolate chips • shredded sweetened coconut • white chocolate chips.

Pumpkin Brownies

Makes sixteen 2¼ × 2¼-inch brownies

These brownies taste somewhat like that autumnal favorite, pumpkin bread—only with chocolate, of course. But don't wait for the crisp days of October to try these treats—make them any time of the year and curl up with a cup of hot tea and a good book, even if the air conditioner is blasting because the oven's been on.

¾ cup unsweetened cocoa powder, sifted
½ cup all-purpose flour, plus additional for the pan
2 teaspoons ground cinnamon
½ teaspoon baking powder
½ teaspoon grated nutmeg
½ teaspoon salt
1 cup packed light brown sugar
6 tablespoons (¾ stick) unsalted butter, plus
  additional for the pan, at room temperature
2 large eggs, at room temperature
One 15-ounce can pumpkin (about 1½ cups)

1. Position the rack in the lower third of the oven. Preheat the oven to 350°F. Butter and flour a 9-inch square baking pan; set it aside.

2. In a medium bowl, whisk the cocoa powder, flour, cinnamon, baking powder, nutmeg, and salt until well combined. Set aside.

3. In a large bowl, cream the brown sugar and butter with an electric mixer at medium speed;

continue beating until the mixture is a pale brown and thick, about 5 minutes. Beat in the eggs one at a time, adding the second only after the first is thoroughly incorporated. Add the canned pumpkin and continue beating at medium speed until smooth and creamy, about 3 minutes.

4. With a wooden spoon or a rubber spatula, stir in the flour mixture just until incorporated. Do not beat. Pour the batter into the prepared pan, spreading it gently to the corners.

5. Bake for 30 minutes, or until a toothpick or cake tester comes out clean. Set the pan on a wire rack to cool for at least 30 minutes.

6. Cut the brownies into 16 squares while they're still in the pan. Carefully remove them with an offset spatula. Serve immediately, or let cool completely before covering with plastic wrap for storage at room temperature. They will stay fresh for up to 4 days. The brownies can be tightly wrapped in wax paper, sealed in a freezer-safe bag, and frozen for up to 4 months; allow them to thaw at room temperature before serving.

To vary this recipe
Add one of the following flavorings with the pumpkin:

2 teaspoons vanilla extract • 1 teaspoon al-mond extract • 1 teaspoon butter flavoring • 1 teaspoon maple extract • 1 teaspoon rum extract

and/or

Stir in ¾ cup of any of the following mix-ins, or ¾ cup any combination of the following mix-ins, with the flour mixture:

chopped banana chips • chopped Butterfinger bars • chopped dried apples • chopped dried apricots • chopped dried pineapple • chopped dried prunes • chopped Heath bars • chopped pecans • chopped walnuts • cocoa nibs • dried cranberries • milk chocolate chips • mini marshmallows • Reese's Pieces • semisweet chocolate chips • white chocolate chips.

Sour Cream Brownies

Makes twenty-four 2¼ × 2⅛-inch brownies

Although decadent to the nth degree, these brownies are actually light because the sour cream leavens the batter, causing them to rise up high in the pan. Ice them with Brown Sugar Icing (page 148), Cola Icing (page 154), or Marshmallow Cream Frosting (page 160).

1½ cups all-purpose flour, plus additional for the pan

1 teaspoon baking soda

½ teaspoon salt

10 tablespoons (1 stick plus 2 tablespoons) unsalted butter, plus additional for the pan, at room temperature

6 ounces bittersweet or semisweet chocolate, chopped, or semisweet chocolate chips

4 ounces unsweetened chocolate, chopped

1¾ cups sugar

½ cup sour cream (regular or low-fat, but not fat-free)

3 large eggs, at room temperature

1 tablespoon vanilla extract

1. Position the rack in the lower third of the oven. Preheat the oven to 350°F. Butter and flour a 9 × 13-inch baking pan; set it aside.

2. In a medium bowl, whisk the flour, baking soda, and salt until well combined. Set aside.

3. Place the butter and both kinds of chocolate in the top of a double boiler set over simmering water. If you don't have a double boiler, place the butter and both kinds of chocolate in a heat-safe bowl that fits snugly over a small pot of simmering water. Stir constantly until half the butter and chocolate is melted. Remove the top of the double boiler or the bowl from the pot; then continue stirring, away from the heat, until the butter and chocolate are completely melted. Transfer the mixture to a large bowl and allow to cool for 10 minutes. (To melt butter and chocolate in a microwave, see pages 9-10.)

4. Beat the sugar into the melted chocolate mixture with a whisk or an electric mixer on medium speed; continue beating until smooth and silky, about 5 minutes by hand or 2 minutes with a mixer. Add the sour cream and beat for 2 minutes. Then beat in the eggs one at a time, making sure each is fully incorporated before adding the next. After beating in the third egg for 1 minute, beat in the vanilla.

5. With a wooden spoon or a rubber spatula, stir in the flour mixture just until combined. Do not beat. Pour the batter into the prepared pan, spreading it gently to the corners.

6. Bake for 35 minutes, or until a toothpick or cake tester comes out clean. Set the pan on a wire rack to cool for at least 30 minutes.

7. Cut the brownies into 24 pieces while they're still in the pan. Carefully remove them with an offset spatula. Serve immediately, or let cool completely before covering with plastic wrap for storage at room temperature. They will stay fresh for up to 4 days. The brownies can be tightly wrapped in wax paper, sealed in a freezer-safe bag, and frozen for up to 4 months; allow them to thaw at room temperature before serving.

To vary this recipe
Whisk 2 teaspoons ground ginger into the flour mixture
and/or
Substitute 1 teaspoon almond extract for the vanilla
and/or
Stir in 1¼ cups of any of the following mix-ins, or 1¼ cups any combination of the following mix-ins, with the flour mixture:
chopped candied chestnuts • chopped honey-roasted almonds • chopped pecans • chopped walnuts • cocoa nibs • dried cranberries • dried currants • semisweet chocolate chips.

Sweet Corn Brownies

Makes twenty-four 2¼ × 2⅛-inch brownies

In the 1930s, a recipe for a chocolate cake made with cream-style corn spread around the country, popularized by a mail-order business that specialized in a monthly set of recipe cards. The brownies we developed from that long-ago favorite are simple, cakey, and made with only unsweetened cocoa powder—the canned corn adds most of the sweetness and moisture. To that end, use only cream-style corn, not niblets. If you want, ice these brownies with Buttercream (page 150) or Cream Cheese Frosting (page 155).

1 cup all-purpose flour, plus additional for the pan
½ cup unsweetened cocoa powder, sifted
2 teaspoons baking powder
8 tablespoons (1 stick) unsalted butter, plus additional for the pan, at room temperature
1 cup sugar
2 large eggs, at room temperature
2 teaspoons vanilla extract
One 14¾-ounce can cream-style corn

1. Position the rack in the lower third of the oven. Preheat the oven to 350°F. Butter and flour a 9 × 13-inch baking pan; set it aside.

2. In a medium bowl, whisk the flour, cocoa powder, and baking powder until well combined. Set aside.

3. In a large bowl, cream the butter and sugar with an electric mixer at medium speed; continue beating until pale yellow and thick, about 5 minutes. Beat in the eggs one at a time, allowing the first to be thoroughly incorporated before adding the second; then beat in the vanilla.

4. Beat in the cream-style corn and the flour mixture, alternating in two additions each, as follows: corn, flour, corn, flour. Beat for another 2 minutes at medium speed until well combined, scraping down the sides of the bowl as necessary. Pour the batter into the prepared pan, spreading it gently to the corners.

5. Bake for 25 minutes, or until a toothpick or cake tester comes out fairly damp, with many moist crumbs attached. The middle of the cake may not be fully set. Set the pan on a wire rack to cool for at least 2 hours.

6. Cut the brownies into 24 pieces while they're still in the pan. Carefully remove them with an offset spatula. Serve immediately, or cover with plastic wrap for storage at room temperature. They will stay fresh for up to 3 days. The brownies can be tightly wrapped in wax paper, sealed in a freezer-safe bag, and frozen for up to 2 months; allow them to thaw at room temperature before serving.

To vary this recipe

Add 1 tablespoon pure chile powder with the flour

and/or

Substitute 2 teaspoons maple extract for the vanilla

and/or

Stir in 1¼ cups of any of the following mix-ins, or 1¼ cups any combination of the following mix-ins, with the flour mixture:

chopped Butterfinger bars • chopped pecans • chopped walnuts • granola • semisweet chocolate chips • shredded sweetened coconut • unsalted shelled sunflower seeds.

Sweet Potato Brownies

Makes sixteen 2¼ × 2¼-inch brownies

These are somewhat like Pumpkin Brownies (page 96), only denser, like a hearty quick bread. Bake the sweet potato on a cookie sheet in a preheated 400°F oven for 50 minutes, or until it is easily pierced with a fork. Cool it completely before proceeding with the recipe. Try these brownies with Cream Cheese Frosting (page 155), Mocha Cream Frosting (page 162), or Vanilla Icing (page 166).

½ cup all-purpose flour, plus additional for the pan

½ cup unsweetened cocoa powder, sifted

1 teaspoon baking powder

1 teaspoon ground cinnamon

½ teaspoon salt

¼ teaspoon grated nutmeg

8 tablespoons (1 stick) unsalted butter, plus additional for the pan, at room temperature

1 cup packed dark brown sugar

1 medium sweet potato, about ½ pound, baked until tender, cooled, peeled, and mashed (see headnote)

1 large egg, at room temperature

1 large egg yolk, at room temperature

1 tablespoon vanilla extract

1. Position the rack in the lower third of the oven. Preheat the oven to 350°F. Butter and flour a 9-inch square baking pan; set it aside.

2. In a medium bowl, whisk the flour, cocoa powder, baking powder, cinnamon, salt, and nutmeg until well combined. Set aside.

3. In a large mixing bowl, cream the butter and brown sugar with an electric mixer at medium speed; continue beating until pale yellow and thick, about 5 minutes. Beat in the mashed sweet potato until the mixture is creamy and smooth, about 2 minutes. Beat in the egg, egg yolk, and vanilla just until incorporated.

4. With a wooden spoon or a rubber spatula, stir in the flour mixture just until combined. Do not beat. Spoon the batter into the prepared pan, spreading it gently to the corners.

5. Bake for 20 minutes, or until a toothpick or cake tester comes out with a few moist crumbs attached. Set the pan on a wire rack to cool for at least 30 minutes.

6. Cut the brownies into 16 squares while they're still in the pan. Carefully remove them with an offset spatula. Serve immediately, or let cool completely before covering with plastic wrap for storage at room temperature. They will stay fresh for up to 3 days. The brownies can be tightly wrapped in wax paper, sealed in a freezer-safe bag, and frozen for up to 3 months; allow them to thaw at room temperature before serving.

To vary this recipe

Whisk 1 teaspoon ground ginger • or 1 teaspoon ground mace into the flour mixture

and/or

Substitute one of the following flavorings for the vanilla:

1½ teaspoons maple extract • 1½ teaspoons rum extract • 1 teaspoon orange extract

and/or

Stir in ¾ cup of any of the following mix-ins, or ¾ cup any combination of the following mix-ins, with the flour mixture:

butterscotch chips • chopped dates • chopped dried figs • chopped dried prunes • chopped pecans • chopped walnuts • cocoa nibs • dried cranberries • dried currants • mini marshmallows • raisins • semisweet chocolate chips • toasted pepitás • white chocolate chips.

Walnut Brownies

Makes twenty-four 2¼ × 2⅛-inch brownies

So fudgy, these brownies are the perfect foil for walnuts. The fat used here is walnut oil, a fairly heart-healthy alternative to butter; it can be found in most supermarkets and gourmet stores. Keep it refrigerated to maximize its shelf-life (it will cloud from the cold), and always smell it to make sure it's still fresh. Serve these brownies with Ganache Icing (page 157) or with Lemon Curd (page 159), used either as an icing or as an accompaniment.

1 cup walnut halves
¾ cup unsweetened cocoa powder, sifted
½ cup all-purpose flour
1 teaspoon baking powder
½ teaspoon salt
1½ cups sugar
¾ cup walnut oil, plus additional for the pan
2 teaspoons vanilla extract
3 large eggs, at room temperature

1. Position the rack in the lower third of the oven. Preheat the oven to 350°F. Using walnut oil, oil a 9 × 13-inch baking pan; set it aside.

2. Grind the walnut halves in a food processor until finely powdered but not a paste. In a large bowl, whisk the ground walnuts with the cocoa powder, flour, baking powder, and salt until well combined. Set aside.

3. In a second large bowl, beat the sugar and walnut oil with an electric mixer at medium speed; continue beating until the sugar has dissolved and the mixture is thick and smooth, about 5 minutes, scraping down the sides of the bowl as necessary. Beat in the vanilla and then the eggs all at once at low speed, just until incorporated, perhaps 10 seconds but no more (otherwise you'll end up with a mayonnaise-like sauce).

4. With a wooden spoon or a rubber spatula, stir in the flour mixture just until incorporated. Do not beat. Spoon the batter into the prepared pan, spreading it gently to the corners.

5. Bake for 25 minutes, or until a toothpick or cake tester comes out with a few crumbs attached. Set the pan on a wire rack to cool for at least 1 hour. (You may also underbake these brownies by a few minutes, taking them out of the oven when the center is still soft. Cool the pan on a wire rack for at least 2 hours, allowing them to fall and become extra fudgy.)

6. Cut the brownies into 24 pieces while they're still in the pan. Carefully remove them with an offset spatula. Serve immediately, or let cool completely before covering with plastic wrap for storage at room temperature. They will stay fresh for up to 4 days. The brownies may be tightly wrapped in wax paper, sealed in a freezer-safe bag, and frozen for up to 3 months; allow them to thaw at room temperature before serving.

To vary this recipe
Whisk one or more of the following spices into the flour mixture:
2 teaspoons ground cinnamon • 2 teaspoons ground ginger • 1 teaspoon ground mace

and/or
Stir in 1¼ cups of any of the following mix-ins, or 1¼ cups any combination of the following mix-ins, with the flour mixture:
chopped dried apples • chopped dried figs • chopped honey-roasted walnuts • cocoa nibs • dried cherries • dried currants • milk chocolate chips • mint chocolate chips • Raisinets • raisins • raspberry chocolate chips • semisweet chocolate chips • white chocolate chips.

White Chocolate Brownies

Makes sixteen 2¼ × 2¼-inch brownies

Even if you're one of those chocolate aficionados who thinks white chocolate isn't truly chocolate, don't turn away from this recipe. First off, these brownies are not white at all—they're dark and rich, thanks to the cocoa powder. The white chocolate adds lots of cocoa butter without any cocoa solids, so the brownies' texture is very smooth—and the chocolate taste is very concentrated. You might be converted to white chocolate yet!

¾ cup unsweetened cocoa powder, sifted

⅔ cup all-purpose flour, plus additional for the pan

1 teaspoon baking soda

½ teaspoon salt

8 ounces white chocolate, chopped, or white chocolate chips

8 tablespoons (1 stick) unsalted butter, plus additional for the pan, at room temperature

⅔ cup sugar

2 large eggs, at room temperature

1 teaspoon vanilla extract

1. Position the rack in the lower third of the oven. Preheat the oven to 350°F. Butter and flour a 9-inch baking pan; set it aside.

2. In a medium bowl, whisk together the cocoa powder, flour, baking soda, and salt until well combined. Set aside.

3. Place the white chocolate in the top half of a double boiler set over simmering water. If you don't have a double boiler, place the white chocolate in a heat-safe bowl that fits snugly over a small pot of simmering water. Stir constantly until half the chocolate is melted. Remove the top of the double boiler or the bowl from the pot; then continue stirring, away from the heat, until the chocolate is completely melted. Allow to cool for 10 minutes. (To melt chocolate in a microwave, see pages 9-10.)

4. In a large bowl, cream the butter and sugar with an electric mixer at medium speed; continue beating until pale yellow and thick, about 5 minutes. Beat in the eggs one at a time, allowing the first to be thoroughly incorporated before adding the second. After beating in the second egg for 1 minute, beat in the vanilla and cooled chocolate mixture until smooth, about 2 minutes, scraping down the sides of the bowl as necessary.

5. With a wooden spoon or a rubber spatula, stir in the flour mixture just until incorporated. Do not beat. Pour the batter into the prepared pan, spreading it gently to the corners.

6. Bake for 20 minutes, or until the cake is set but still soft in the center. Set the pan on a wire rack to cool for at least 2 hours. The brownies will fall as they firm up.

7. Cut the brownies into 16 squares while they're still in the pan. Carefully remove them with an offset spatula. Serve immediately, or cover with plastic wrap for storage at room temperature. They will stay fresh for up to 4 days. The brownies may be tightly wrapped in wax paper, sealed in a freezer-safe bag, and frozen for up to 3 months; allow them to thaw at room temperature before serving.

To vary this recipe

Add one of the following flavorings with the vanilla:

1 teaspoon almond extract • 1 teaspoon banana extract • 1 teaspoon coconut extract • 1 teaspoon maple extract • 1 teaspoon mint extract • 1 teaspoon orange extract • 1 teaspoon rum extract

and/or

Stir in ¾ cup of any of the following mix-ins, or ¾ cup any combination of the following mix-ins, with the flour mixture:

chopped candied chestnuts • chopped dried apricots • chopped pecans • chopped toasted chickpeas • chopped toasted hazelnuts • chopped unsalted cashews • chopped unsalted roasted peanuts • chopped walnuts • cocoa nibs • granola • plain or chocolate-covered espresso beans • raisins.

Yogurt Brownies

Makes sixteen 2 × 2-inch brownies

These are among the easiest brownies in the book—you don't have to melt chocolate, temper eggs, or cream butter and sugar. Instead, the yogurt alone ensures richness, leavening, and body. With so much time to spare, you might want to whip up a luscious icing, like the Chocolate Fudge Frosting (page 152).

Unsalted butter for the pan
¾ cup unsweetened cocoa powder, sifted
½ cup all-purpose flour, plus additional for the pan
½ teaspoon baking powder
½ teaspoon salt
¾ cup sugar
½ cup plain yogurt (regular, low-fat, or fat-free)
2 teaspoons vanilla extract

1. Position the rack in the lower third of the oven. Preheat the oven to 350°F. Butter and flour an 8-inch square baking pan; set it aside.

2. In a medium bowl, whisk the cocoa powder, flour, baking powder, and salt until well combined. Set aside.

3. In a large bowl, stir the sugar, yogurt, and vanilla with a wooden spoon until the sugar has dissolved and the mixture is uniform, about 3 minutes. Stir in the flour mixture just until combined. Do not beat. Pour the batter into the prepared pan, spreading it gently to the corners.

4. Bake for 20 minutes, or until a toothpick or cake tester comes out clean. Set the pan on a wire rack to cool for at least 30 minutes.

5. Cut the brownies into 16 squares while they're still in the pan. Carefully remove them with an offset spatula. Serve immediately, or let cool completely before covering with plastic wrap for storage at room temperature. They will stay fresh for up to 3 days. The brownies can be tightly wrapped in wax paper, sealed in a freezer-safe bag, and frozen for up to 2 months; allow them to thaw at room temperature before serving.

To vary this recipe
Whisk 1 tablespoon poppy seeds into the flour mixture
and/or
Stir in ½ cup of any of the following mix-ins, or ½ cup any combination of the following mix-ins, with the flour mixture:
almond M & M's • butterscotch chips • chopped banana chips • chopped Heath bars • chopped honey-roasted almonds • chopped honey-roasted peanuts • chopped pecans • chopped walnuts • cocoa nibs • crumbled Oreo cookies • dried cranberries • mint chocolate chips • peanut butter chips • raisins • Reese's Pieces • semisweet chocolate chips • slivered almonds • unsalted shelled sunflower seeds • yogurt-covered raisins.

Blondies

Almond Blondies

Makes sixteen 2¼ × 2¼-inch blondies

Blondies, by and large, are crunchier than brownies, more like a cookie perhaps, or at least a traditional bar cookie. As we stated in the Introduction, the blondie was actually the original "brownie"—that is, a cake browned in the oven. Only later was chocolate added. But it was an inspired addition—so much so, in fact, that we decided to put chocolate in almost all our blondies, making them a cookie-like dough laced with chips—and in this case, almonds.

¾ cup all-purpose flour, plus additional for the pan
½ teaspoon baking powder
¼ teaspoon salt
8 tablespoons (1 stick) unsalted butter, plus additional for the pan, at room temperature
½ cup packed light brown sugar
½ cup granulated sugar
2 large eggs, at room temperature
1 teaspoon vanilla extract
1 teaspoon almond extract
2 cups sliced almonds

3 ounces semisweet chocolate chips (about ½ cup), or chopped semisweet or bittersweet chocolate

1. Position the rack in the lower third of the oven. Preheat the oven to 350°F. Butter and flour a 9-inch square baking pan; set it aside.

2. In a medium bowl, whisk the flour, baking powder, and salt until well combined. Set aside.

3. In a large bowl, cream the butter, brown sugar, and granulated sugar with an electric mixer at medium speed; continue beating until pale brown and very thick, about 4 minutes. Add the eggs one at a time, allowing the first to be thoroughly incorporated before adding the second. Scrape down the sides of the bowl as necessary. After beating in the second egg for 1 minute, beat in the vanilla and almond extracts.

4. With a wooden spoon or a rubber spatula, stir in the sliced almonds and the chocolate chips until well combined. The batter will be very thick. Stir in the flour mixture just until incorporated. Do not beat. Spoon the batter into the prepared pan, spreading it gently to the corners.

5. Bake for 45 minutes, or until the top is light brown and a toothpick or cake tester comes out with a few moist crumbs attached. Set the pan on a wire rack to cool for at least 30 minutes.

6. Cut the blondies into 16 squares while they're still in the pan. Carefully remove them with an offset spatula. Serve immediately, or let cool completely before covering with plastic wrap for storage at room temperature. They will stay fresh for up to 3 days. The blondies can be tightly wrapped in wax paper, sealed in a freezer-safe bag, and frozen for up to 3 months; allow them to thaw at room temperature before serving.

To vary this recipe

Add ½ teaspoon grated nutmeg • ½ teaspoon ground mace • and/or ½ teaspoon ground cloves to the flour mixture

and/or

Add 1 teaspoon maple extract with the vanilla

and/or

Substitute butterscotch chips • milk chocolate chips • or white chocolate chips for the semisweet chocolate chips

and/or

Stir in ¾ cup of any of the following mix-ins, or ¾ cup any combination of the following mix-ins, with the chocolate chips:

chopped banana chips • chopped dried pineapple • cocoa nibs • dried blueberries • dried cherries • dried cranberries • dried currants • unsalted shelled sunflower seeds.

Banana Blondies

Makes twenty-four 2¼ × 2⅛-inch blondies

This moist blondie takes its banana flavor from both fresh bananas and banana chips (see page 5). For best results, the fresh banana should be very ripe, even slightly soft, with brown spots on the peel. If you prefer a denser, chewier blondie, rap the pan on the oven rack after 15 minutes' baking time.

2¼ cups all-purpose flour, plus additional for the pan
1 teaspoon ground cinnamon
1 teaspoon baking powder
½ teaspoon salt
10 tablespoons (1 stick plus 2 tablespoons) unsalted butter, plus additional for the pan, at room temperature
1 cup granulated sugar
1 cup packed light brown sugar
1 ripe banana, peeled and cut into ½-inch chunks
2 large eggs, at room temperature
1 large egg yolk, at room temperature
2 teaspoons vanilla extract
2 cups coarsely chopped banana chips (about 7 ounces)
6 ounces semisweet chocolate chips (about 1 cup), or chopped semisweet or bittersweet chocolate

1. Position the rack in the lower third of the oven. Preheat the oven to 350°F. Butter and flour a 9 × 13-inch baking pan; set it aside.

2. In a medium bowl, whisk the flour, cinnamon, baking powder, and salt until well combined. Set aside.

3. In a large bowl, cream the butter, granulated sugar, and brown sugar with an electric mixer at medium speed; continue beating until pale brown and very thick, about 6 minutes. Beat in the banana chunks until the batter is smooth. Then add the eggs one at a time, allowing each to be thoroughly incorporated before adding the next. Scrape down the sides of the bowl as necessary, then beat in the egg yolk and the vanilla.

4. With a wooden spoon or a rubber spatula, stir in the banana chips and chocolate chips until well combined. Then stir in the flour mixture just until incorporated. Do not beat. Spoon the batter into the prepared pan, spreading it gently to the corners.

5. Bake for 35 minutes, or until the top is light brown and a toothpick or cake tester comes out clean. Set the pan on a wire rack to cool for at least 30 minutes.

6. Cut the blondies into 24 pieces while they're still in the pan. Carefully remove them with an offset spatula. Serve immediately, or let cool completely before covering with plastic wrap for storage at room temperature. They will stay fresh for up to 3 days. The blondies can be tightly wrapped in wax paper, sealed in a freezer-safe bag, and frozen for up to 3 months; allow them to thaw at room temperature before serving.

To vary this recipe
Add one of the following flavorings with the vanilla:
1½ teaspoons rum extract • 1½ teaspoons maple extract • 1 teaspoon almond extract
and/or
Substitute butterscotch chips • milk chocolate chips • peanut butter chips • or white chocolate chips for the semisweet chocolate chips

and/or
Stir in 1¼ cups of any of the following mix-ins, or 1¼ cups any combination of the following mix-ins, with the chocolate chips:
chopped dried figs • chopped pecans • chopped walnuts • cocoa nibs • crumbled biscotti • crumbled molasses cookies • dried cherries • dried cranberries • dried strawberries • honey-roasted peanuts • mini marshmallows • peanut butter chips • peanut M & M's • slivered almonds.

Blondies in a Jar

Makes 1 quart of blondie mix for one 9-inch square pan of blondies

Like Brownies in a Jar (page 27), this gift idea is perfect for housewarmings, birthdays, or the holidays. Because of the walnuts, however, it has a more limited shelf-life—perhaps just a month or so. Decorate the jar and use fabric instead of a canning lid, securing the fabric with ribbon or with the screw-top ring of the traditional canning lid. The blondie recipe card is given below the variations—be sure you include it with the gift.

One-quart canning jar or 1-quart decorative jar, plus a lid
½ cup granulated sugar
1 cup all-purpose flour
1½ teaspoons baking powder
¾ teaspoon salt
1 cup packed light brown sugar
1 cup chopped walnuts
½ cup semisweet chocolate chips

1. Carefully pour the granulated sugar into the jar, gently rapping the jar against the counter to get an even layer of sugar. Wipe the inside of the jar with a dry paper towel to clean off any dust.

2. In a medium bowl, whisk the flour, baking powder, and salt until well combined. Carefully spoon the mixture into the jar, gently tamping it down and wiping the inside of the jar with a clean, dry paper towel.

3. Spoon the brown sugar into the jar; add the walnuts, then the chocolate chips. Seal with a canning lid and ring, or with a decorative lid.

To vary this recipe
Substitute 1 cup of any of the following for the walnuts:
chopped pecans • chopped toasted hazelnuts • cocoa nibs • toasted pepitás • slivered almonds
and/or
Substitute ½ cup of any of the following for the chocolate chips:
butterscotch chips • M & M's • milk chocolate chips • mint chocolate chips • peanut butter chips • Reese's Pieces • white chocolate chips.

Blondie Mix Recipe Card

Preheat the oven to 350°F. Grease or butter and flour a 9-inch square baking pan. Empty the blondie mix into a large bowl. Add 6 tablespoons unsalted butter or margarine, melted and cooled, 2 teaspoons vanilla extract, and 2 large eggs, well beaten. Mix well and spread into the pan. Bake for 35 minutes or until a toothpick comes out with a few moist crumbs attached. Cool completely in the pan before cutting.

Butterscotch Blondies

Makes twenty-four 2¼ × 2⅛-inch blondies

Chocolate-less, these blondies are crisper and more compact, much more like bar cookies, than some of the others. The crunchy texture works well against the sweet butterscotch chips. If you still want chocolate, ice these blondies with Chocolate Fudge Frosting (page 152) or Ganache Icing (page 157).

1⅔ cups butterscotch chips (about an 11-ounce package)
6 tablespoons (¾ stick) unsalted butter, plus additional for the pan, at room temperature
2 cups all-purpose flour, plus additional for the pan
1 teaspoon baking powder
1 teaspoon salt
¼ teaspoon baking soda
1 cup granulated sugar
1 cup packed light brown sugar
3 large eggs, at room temperature
2 teaspoons vanilla extract

1. Position the rack in the lower third of the oven. Preheat the oven to 350°F. Butter and flour a 9 × 13-inch baking pan; set it aside.

2. Place ⅔ cup butterscotch chips and the butter in the top of a double boiler set over simmering water. If you don't have a double boiler, place ⅔ cup butterscotch chips and the butter in a heat-safe bowl that fits snugly over a small pot of simmering water. Stir constantly until half the chips and butter is melted. Remove the top of the double boiler or the bowl from over the pot. Continue stirring, away from the heat, until the chips and butter are completely melted; allow to cool for 10 minutes. The mixture may separate, but it will reincorporate in the batter.

3. Meanwhile, whisk the flour, baking powder, salt, and baking soda in a medium bowl until well combined. Set aside.

4. In a large bowl, beat the granulated sugar, brown sugar, and eggs with an electric mixer at medium speed; continue beating until the sugar has dissolved, about 5 minutes, scraping down the sides of the bowl as necessary. Beat in the butterscotch mixture and the vanilla until smooth and uniform, about 2 minutes.

5. With a wooden spoon or a rubber spatula, stir in first the remaining 1 cup butterscotch chips, then the flour mixture, just until incorporated. Do not beat. The batter will be very thick. Spoon it into the prepared pan, spreading it gently to the corners.

6. Bake for 35 minutes, or until the top is light brown and a toothpick or cake tester comes out with a few moist crumbs attached. Set the pan on a wire rack to cool for at least 30 minutes.

7. Cut the blondies into 24 pieces while they're still in the pan. Carefully remove them with an offset spatula. Serve immediately, or let cool completely before covering with plastic wrap for storage at room temperature. They will stay fresh for up to 3 days. The blondies can be tightly wrapped in wax paper, sealed in a freezer-safe bag, and frozen for up to 3 months; allow them to thaw at room temperature before serving.

To vary this recipe
Add 2 teaspoons ground cinnamon • and/or 2 teaspoons ground ginger to the flour mixture

and/or
Add 1½ teaspoons maple extract • or 1½ teaspoons rum extract with the vanilla

and/or
Stir in 1¼ cups of any of the following mix-ins, or 1¼ cups any combination of the following mix-ins, with the unmelted butterscotch chips: chopped Butterfinger bars • chopped Heath bars • chopped pecans • chopped toasted hazelnuts • chopped walnuts • dried cherries • dried cranberries • Goobers • mini marshmallows • peanut M & M's.

Carrot Blondies

Makes twenty-four 2¼ × 2⅛-inch blondies

These treats are a cross between carrot cake and traditional blondies; they rise up quite high in the pan and are very light. They're especially good with a cup of hot tea, or even as an on-the-run breakfast. Shred the carrots with a box grater, or in a food processor with the shredding blade attached. Carrot Blondies are best topped with Cream Cheese Frosting (page 155).

3½ cups all-purpose flour

2 teaspoons baking soda

1 teaspoon ground cinnamon

1 teaspoon salt

½ teaspoon ground ginger

½ teaspoon grated nutmeg

1 cup canola or vegetable oil, plus additional for the pan

1 cup packed dark brown sugar

½ cup granulated sugar

3 large eggs, at room temperature

1 teaspoon vanilla extract

3 cups shredded carrot (about 1 pound carrots)

6 ounces semisweet chocolate chips (about 1 cup), or chopped semisweet or bittersweet chocolate

1. Position the rack in the lower third of the oven. Preheat the oven to 350°F. Oil a 9 × 13-inch baking pan; set it aside.

2. In a medium bowl, whisk the flour, baking soda, cinnamon, salt, ginger, and nutmeg until well combined. Set aside.

3. In a large bowl, beat the oil, brown sugar, and granulated sugar with an electric mixer at medium speed; continue beating until the sugars have dissolved, about 5 minutes. Add the eggs one at a time, allowing each to be thoroughly incorporated before adding the next. Scrape down the sides of the bowl as necessary. After beating in the third egg for 1 minute, stir in the vanilla.

4. With a wooden spoon or a rubber spatula, stir in the shredded carrot and the chocolate chips until well combined. Then stir in the flour mixture just until incorporated. Do not beat. Spoon the batter into the prepared pan, spreading it gently to the corners.

5. Bake for 35 minutes, or until the top is light brown and a toothpick or cake tester comes out with a few moist crumbs attached. Set the pan on a wire rack to cool for at least 30 minutes.

6. Cut the blondies into 24 pieces while they're still in the pan. Carefully remove them with an offset spatula. Serve immediately, or let cool completely before covering with plastic wrap for storage at room temperature. They will stay fresh for up to 4 days. The blondies can be tightly wrapped in wax paper, sealed in a freezer-safe bag, and frozen for up to 3 months; allow them to thaw at room temperature before serving.

To vary this recipe

Substitute 1½ teaspoons rum extract for the vanilla

and/or

Add 2 teaspoons finely grated orange zest with the shredded carrot

and/or

Substitute milk chocolate chips • or white chocolate chips for the semisweet chocolate chips

and/or

Stir in 1¼ cups of any of the following mix-ins, or 1¼ cups any combination of the following mix-ins, with the chocolate chips:

chopped dried figs • chopped dried pineapple • chopped dried prunes • chopped pecans • chopped walnuts • crumbled biscotti • dried currants • granola • yellow raisins.

Classic Blondies

Makes twenty-four 2¼ × 2⅛-inch blondies

Look no further for the real thing: a thick, chewy, yet still cakey blondie. These taste like chocolate chip cookie dough—even after they're baked! If you leave them out on the counter uncovered for 24 hours, they turn slightly stale and are then excellent mixed into homemade ice cream for the last minute of churning. For the best ice cream flavors, make sure you check out *The Ultimate Ice Cream Book*.

3 cups all-purpose flour, plus additional for the pan
2 teaspoons baking powder
½ teaspoon salt
¾ pound (3 sticks) unsalted butter, plus additional for the pan, at room temperature
1⅔ cups granulated sugar
1 cup packed light brown sugar
4 large eggs, at room temperature
2 tablespoons vanilla extract
6 ounces semisweet chocolate chips (about 1 cup), or chopped semisweet or bittersweet chocolate

1. Position the rack in the lower third of the oven. Preheat the oven to 350°F. Butter and flour a 9 × 13-inch baking pan; set it aside.

2. In a medium bowl, whisk the flour, baking powder, and salt until well combined. Set aside.

3. In a large bowl, cream the butter, granulated sugar, and brown sugar with an electric mixer at medium speed; continue beating until pale brown and thick, about 7 minutes. Add the eggs one at a time, allowing each to be thoroughly incorporated before adding the next. Scrape down the sides of the bowl as necessary. After beating in the fourth egg for 1 minute, beat in the vanilla.

4. With a wooden spoon or a rubber spatula, stir in first the chocolate chips, then the flour mixture, just until incorporated. Do not beat, although the batter will be very thick. Spoon the batter into the prepared pan, spreading it gently to the corners.

5. Bake for 45 minutes, or until the top is light brown and a toothpick or cake tester comes out with a few moist crumbs attached. Set the pan on a wire rack to cool for at least 30 minutes.

6. Cut the blondies into 24 pieces while they're still in the pan. Carefully remove them with an offset spatula. Serve immediately, or let cool completely before covering with plastic wrap for storage at room temperature. They will stay fresh for up to 3 days. The blondies can be tightly wrapped in wax paper, sealed in a freezer-safe bag, and frozen for up to 2 months; allow them to thaw at room temperature before serving.

To vary this recipe

Add one or more of the following spices to the flour mixture:

2 teaspoons ground cinnamon • 2 teaspoons ground ginger • 1 teaspoon ground mace • ½ teaspoon grated nutmeg

and/or

Add one of the following flavorings with the vanilla:

2 teaspoons banana extract • 2 teaspoons banana extract • 2 teaspoons maple extract • 2 teaspoons orange extract • 2 teaspoons rum extract • 1½ teaspoons almond extract

and/or

Substitute butterscotch chips • milk chocolate chips • mint chocolate chips • peanut butter chips • or white chocolate chips for the semi-sweet chocolate chips

and/or

Stir in 1¼ cups of any of the following mix-ins, or 1¼ cups any combination of the following mix-ins, with the chocolate chips:

chopped dried apricots • chopped honey-roasted almonds • chopped honey-roasted peanuts • chopped pecans • chopped toasted hazelnuts • chopped walnuts • cocoa nibs • dried cherries • dried currants • pinenuts • raisins • slivered almonds.

Coconut Blondies

Makes sixteen 2¼ × 2¼-inch blondies

Because the coconut and chocolate chips are so heavy, there's an extra egg white in these blondies to lighten the batter. The result is quite crunchy, like a macaroon. They need at least an hour to cool and set up before they're ready. Good on their own, they're superb topped with Cocoa Frosting (page 153). Unsweetened coconut flakes are available in most gourmet stores and health-food markets.

1 cup all-purpose flour, plus additional for the pan

½ teaspoon baking powder

½ teaspoon salt

8 tablespoons (1 stick) unsalted butter, plus additional for the pan, at room temperature

¾ cup packed light brown sugar

½ cup granulated sugar

1 large egg, at room temperature

1 large egg white, at room temperature

1 teaspoon vanilla extract

2 cups unsweetened coconut flakes (about 4 ounces)

3 ounces semisweet chocolate chips (about ½ cup), or chopped semisweet or bittersweet chocolate

1. Position the rack in the lower third of the oven. Preheat the oven to 350°F. Butter and flour a 9-inch square baking pan; set it aside.

2. In a medium bowl, whisk the flour, baking powder, and salt until well combined. Set aside.

3. In a large bowl, cream the butter, brown sugar, and granulated sugar with an electric mixer at medium speed; continue beating until pale brown and thick, about 5 minutes. Beat in the egg, allowing it to be thoroughly incorporated before beating in the egg white, vanilla, and coconut flakes. Beat for an additional 2 minutes, scraping down the sides of the bowl as necessary.

4. With a wooden spoon or a rubber spatula, stir in the chocolate chips until well combined; then stir in the dry ingredients just until incorporated. Do not beat. Spoon the batter into the prepared pan, spreading it gently to the corners.

5. Bake for 25 minutes, or until the top is light brown and a toothpick or cake tester comes out with a few moist crumbs attached. Set the pan on a wire rack to cool for at least 1 hour.

6. Cut the blondies into 16 squares while they're still in the pan. Carefully remove them with an offset spatula. Serve immediately, or let cool completely before covering with plastic wrap for storage at room temperature. They will stay fresh for up to 4 days. The blondies can be tightly wrapped in wax paper, sealed in a freezer-safe bag, and frozen for up to 3 months; allow them to thaw at room temperature before serving.

To vary this recipe
Substitute 1½ teaspoons banana extract • or 1½ teaspoons rum extract for the vanilla
and/or
Double the semisweet chocolate chips to 6 ounces
and/or
Substitute milk chocolate chips • peanut butter chips • or white chocolate chips for the semisweet chocolate chips

and/or
Stir in 1¼ cups of any of the following mix-ins, or 1¼ cups any combination of the following mix-ins, with the chocolate chips:
chopped dried mango • chopped dried papaya • chopped dried pineapple • chopped walnuts • cocoa nibs • dried cherries • granola • raisins • slivered almonds.

Coffee Blondies

Makes twenty-four 2¼ × 2⅛-inch blondies

These perk-you-up blondies are thin, almost flat, but still chewy. They're reminiscent of the flat biscuits served in the afternoon with a cup of espresso all across Central Europe. If you want, ice them with Ganache Icing (page 157) or Mocha Cream Frosting (page 162). Or you can enjoy them cold, chewy like a candy bar, straight out of the freezer.

2 tablespoons instant coffee powder

1 tablespoon vanilla extract

1 tablespoon hot water

1¾ cups all-purpose flour, plus additional for the pan

1½ teaspoons baking powder

½ teaspoon salt

2 cups packed dark brown sugar

10 tablespoons (1 stick plus 2 tablespoons) unsalted butter, at room temperature, plus additional for the pan

2 large eggs, at room temperature

6 ounces semisweet chocolate chips (about 1 cup), or chopped semisweet or bittersweet chocolate

1. Position the rack in the lower third of the oven. Preheat the oven to 350°F. Butter and flour a 9 × 13-inch baking pan; set it aside.

2. In a small bowl, stir the instant coffee powder into the vanilla and hot water until the coffee dissolves; set aside. In a medium bowl, whisk the flour, baking powder, and salt until well combined; set aside.

3. In a large bowl, cream the brown sugar and butter with an electric mixer at medium speed; continue beating until smooth and thick, about 6 minutes. Add the eggs one at a time, allowing the first to be thoroughly incorporated before adding the second, scraping down the sides of the bowl as necessary.

4. With a wooden spoon or a rubber spatula, stir in the coffee mixture and the chocolate chips until well combined. Then stir in the flour mixture just until incorporated. Do not beat. Spoon the batter into the prepared pan, spreading it gently to the corners.

5. Bake for 25 minutes, or until the top is light brown and a toothpick or cake tester comes out with a few moist crumbs attached. Set the pan on a wire rack to cool for at least 30 minutes.

6. Cut the blondies into 24 pieces while they're still in the pan. Carefully remove them with an offset spatula. Serve immediately, or let cool completely before covering with plastic wrap for storage at room temperature. They will stay fresh for up to 3 days. The blondies can be tightly wrapped in wax paper, sealed in a freezer-safe bag, and frozen for up to 3 months; allow them to thaw at room temperature before serving.

To vary this recipe

Substitute 2 teaspoons maple extract • or 2 teaspoons rum extract for the vanilla

and/or

Substitute butterscotch chips • or white chocolate chips for the semisweet chocolate chips

and/or

Stir in 1¼ cups of any of the following mix-ins, or 1¼ cups any combination of the following mix-ins, with the chocolate chips:

chocolate-covered espresso beans • chopped candied chestnuts • chopped dates • chopped honey-roasted almonds • chopped pecans • chopped toasted hazelnuts • chopped walnuts • cocoa nibs • crumbled biscotti • dried cherries.

Cream Cheese Blondies

Makes twenty-four 2¼ × 2⅛-inch blondies

These blondies fall while they're baking, becoming chewy treats with that classic, creamy, slightly sour edge. In other words, they're a blondie version of chocolate cheesecake. Too rich for an icing, try them with hot mulled cider or a Canadian Eiswein, a sweet, syrupy dessert wine made from grapes bitten hard by winter frosts, shriveled and concentrated.

2 cups all-purpose flour, plus additional
   for the pan
1 teaspoon baking powder
1 teaspoon salt
8 tablespoons (1 stick) unsalted butter, plus
   additional for the pan, at room temperature
½ pound cream cheese (regular, low-fat, or fat-
   free), softened
1 cup granulated sugar
1 cup packed dark brown sugar
2 large eggs, at room temperature
1 large egg yolk, at room temperature
1 tablespoon vanilla extract
6 ounces semisweet chocolate chips (about 1 cup),
   or chopped semisweet or bittersweet chocolate

1. Position the rack in the lower third of the oven. Preheat the oven to 350°F. Butter and flour a 9 × 13-inch baking pan; set it aside.

2. In a medium bowl, whisk the flour, baking powder, and salt until well combined. Set aside.

3. In a large bowl, cream the butter, cream cheese, granulated sugar, and brown sugar with an electric mixer at medium speed; continue beating until the sugars have dissolved and the mixture is smooth and thick, about 8 minutes. Add the eggs one at a time, allowing the first to be thoroughly incorporated before adding the second. Beat in the egg yolk and vanilla, scraping down the sides of the bowl as necessary.

4. With a wooden spoon or a rubber spatula, stir in the chocolate chips until well combined; then stir in the flour mixture just until incorporated. Do not beat. Spoon the batter into the prepared pan, spreading it gently to the corners.

5. Bake for 45 minutes, or until the top is light brown and a toothpick or cake tester comes out with a few moist crumbs attached. Set the pan on a wire rack to cool for at least 30 minutes.

6. Cut the blondies into 24 pieces while they're still in the pan. Carefully remove them with an offset spatula. Serve immediately, or let cool completely before covering with plastic wrap for storage at room temperature. They will stay fresh for up to 3 days. The blondies can be tightly wrapped in wax paper, sealed in a freezer-safe bag, and frozen for up to 3 months; allow them to thaw at room temperature before serving.

To vary this recipe

Add 2 tablespoons chopped crystallized ginger to the flour mixture

and/or

Add one of the following flavorings with the vanilla:

1 teaspoon almond extract • 1 teaspoon coconut extract • 1 teaspoon maple extract • 1 teaspoon rum extract

and/or

Substitute butterscotch chips • peanut butter chips • or white chocolate chips for the semi-sweet chocolate chips

and/or

Stir in 1¼ cups of any of the following mix-ins, or 1¼ cups any combination of the following mix-ins, with the chocolate chips:

chopped candied chestnuts • chopped candied orange peel • chopped dates • chopped dried apricots • chopped honey-roasted almonds • chopped honey-roasted peanuts • cocoa nibs • crumbled biscotti • dried cherries.

Fruitcake Blondies

Makes sixteen 2¼ × 2¼-inch blondies

The trick to making a good fruitcake (and yes, Virginia, there is a good fruitcake) is to ripen it in rum-soaked towels for up to two months in the refrigerator. This blondie was created to pay homage to that tradition, but with this exception: Fruitcake is traditionally made with glacéed fruit, but this blondie is made with dried fruit that is soaked in rum. Use the leftover rum marinade for cocktails, or spoon it over the blondies as a sauce.

2 cups chopped dried fruit (such as pineapple, papaya, cranberries, apricots, and/or raisins)

1 cup gold rum

1⅓ cups all-purpose flour, plus additional for the pan

1 teaspoon baking powder

1 teaspoon salt

10 tablespoons (1 stick plus 2 tablespoons) unsalted butter, plus additional for the pan, at room temperature

½ cup granulated sugar

½ cup packed dark brown sugar

1 large egg, at room temperature

1 large egg yolk, at room temperature

2 teaspoons vanilla extract

3 ounces semisweet chocolate chips (about ½ cup), or chopped semisweet or bittersweet chocolate

1. Combine the dried fruit and rum in a medium bowl. Set aside to marinate, stirring occasionally, for at least 6 hours or overnight.

2. Position the rack in the lower third of the oven. Preheat the oven to 350°F. Butter and flour a 9-inch square baking pan; set it aside.

3. Drain the fruit; reserve the marinade for another use. In a medium bowl, whisk the flour, baking powder, and salt until well combined. Set aside.

4. In a large bowl, cream the butter, granulated sugar, and brown sugar with an electric mixer at medium speed; continue beating until pale brown and thick, about 6 minutes. Add the egg and beat until thoroughly incorporated; then add the egg yolk and vanilla. Beat an additional 1 minute, scraping down the sides of the bowl as necessary.

5. With a wooden spoon or a rubber spatula, stir in the chocolate chips and the drained fruit until well combined. Then stir in the flour mixture just until incorporated. Do not beat. Spoon the batter into the prepared pan, spreading it gently to the corners.

6. Bake for 25 minutes, or until the top is light brown and a toothpick or cake tester comes out with a few moist crumbs attached. Set the pan on a wire rack to cool for at least 30 minutes.

7. Cut the blondies into 16 squares while they're still in the pan. Carefully remove them with an offset spatula. Serve immediately, or let cool completely before covering with plastic wrap for storage at room temperature. They will stay fresh for up to 4 days. Because of the dried fruit, these blondies do not freeze well.

To vary this recipe
Double the chocolate chips to 6 ounces
and/or
Substitute white chocolate chips for the semi-sweet chocolate chips

and/or
Stir in ¾ cup of any of the following mix-ins, or ¾ cup any combination of the following mix-ins, with the chocolate chips:
chopped pecans • chopped toasted hazelnuts • chopped walnuts • slivered almonds • toasted pepitás.

Gingerbread Blondies

Makes sixteen 2¼ × 2¼-inch blondies

One of the best things about ginger-bread is the way your kitchen smells while it's baking. *One* of the best things, that is, because spicy gingerbread is just as comforting once it's baked. These blondies are light and moist, almost airy. If you want, ice them with Sour Cream Icing (page 165) or the fudgy Five Minute Chocolate Frosting (page 156).

1¾ cups all-purpose flour, plus additional for the pan
2 teaspoons ground ginger
½ teaspoon baking soda
½ teaspoon salt
8 tablespoons (1 stick) unsalted butter, plus additional for the pan, at room temperature
½ cup packed dark brown sugar
½ cup molasses
2 large eggs, at room temperature
6 ounces semisweet chocolate chips (about 1 cup), or chopped semisweet or bittersweet chocolate

1. Position the rack in the lower third of the oven. Preheat the oven to 350°F. Butter and flour a 9-inch square baking pan; set it aside.

2. In a medium bowl, whisk the flour, ginger, baking soda, and salt until well combined. Set aside.

3. In a large bowl, cream the butter and brown sugar with an electric mixer at medium speed; continue beating until pale brown and thick, about 5 minutes. Beat in the molasses until smooth and uniform. Then beat in the eggs one at a time, allowing the first to be thoroughly incorporated before adding the second. Scrape down the sides of the bowl as necessary.

4. With a wooden spoon or a rubber spatula, stir in first the chocolate chips, then the flour mixture, just until incorporated. Do not beat. Spoon the batter into the prepared pan, spreading it gently to the corners.

5. Bake for 20 minutes, or until the top is light brown and a toothpick or cake tester comes out clean. Set the pan on a wire rack to cool for at least 30 minutes.

6. Cut the blondies into 16 squares while they're still in the pan. Carefully remove them with an offset spatula. Serve immediately, or let cool completely before covering with plastic wrap for storage at room temperature. They will stay fresh for up to 2 days. The blondies can be tightly wrapped in wax paper, sealed in a freezer-safe bag, and frozen for up to 3 months; allow them to thaw at room temperature before serving.

To vary this recipe

Substitute 3 tablespoons finely chopped crystallized ginger for the ground ginger

and/or

Add 1 teaspoon ground mace with the ginger

and/or

Substitute white chocolate chips for the semisweet chocolate chips

and/or

Stir in ¾ cup of any of the following mix-ins, or ¾ cup any combination of the following mix-ins, with the chocolate chips:

chopped dried figs • chopped dried prunes • chopped pecans • cocoa nibs • dried cranberries • yellow raisins.

Honey Yogurt Blondies

Makes sixteen 2¼ × 2¼-inch blondies

For these moist, aromatic, sticky blondies, use a strong-flavored honey like wildflower, buckwheat, or even star thistle (see the Source Guide). Because yogurt leavens the batter, these blondies are very light yet fairly compact; they travel well to picnics or family reunions. What's more, they're one of the simplest blondies in the book.

Unsalted butter for the pan
1½ cups all-purpose flour, plus additional for
  the pan
½ teaspoon baking powder
½ teaspoon baking soda
½ teaspoon salt
½ cup plain yogurt (regular, low-fat, or fat-free)
½ cup honey
4 large eggs, at room temperature
1 tablespoon vanilla extract
6 ounces semisweet chocolate chips (about 1 cup),
  or chopped semisweet or bittersweet chocolate

1. Position the rack in the lower third of the oven. Preheat the oven to 350°F. Butter and flour a 9-inch square baking pan; set it aside.

2. In a medium bowl, whisk the flour, baking powder, baking soda, and salt until well combined. Set aside.

3. In a large bowl, beat the yogurt, honey, eggs, and vanilla with an electric mixer at medium speed until smooth and uniform, about 2 minutes. Stir in the chocolate chips.

4. With a wooden spoon or a rubber spatula, stir in the flour mixture just until incorporated. Do not beat, although the batter will be very sticky. Spoon the batter into the prepared pan, spreading it gently to the corners.

5. Bake for 18 minutes, or until the top is light brown and a toothpick or cake tester comes out clean. Set the pan on a wire rack to cool for at least 1 hour.

6. Cut the blondies into 16 squares while they're still in the pan. Carefully remove them with an offset spatula. Serve immediately, or let cool completely before covering with plastic wrap for storage at room temperature. They will stay fresh for up to 2 days. The blondies can be tightly wrapped in wax paper, sealed in a freezer-safe bag, and frozen for up to 2 months; allow them to thaw at room temperature before serving.

To vary this recipe
Add one or more of the following spices to the flour mixture:

1 tablespoon poppy seeds • 2 teaspoons ground cinnamon • 2 teaspoons ground ginger • ½ teaspoon grated nutmeg • ½ teaspoon ground cloves

and/or

Substitute one of the following flavorings for the vanilla:

2 teaspoons maple extract • 1 teaspoon lemon extract • 1 teaspoon mint extract

and/or

Substitute mint chocolate chips • raspberry chocolate chips • or white chocolate chips for the semisweet chocolate chips

and/or

Stir in ¾ cup of any of the following mix-ins, or ¾ cup any combination of the following mix-ins, with the chocolate chips:

chopped dried apples • chopped dried pineapple • chopped pecans • chopped walnuts • dried cherries • dried currants • raisins • shredded sweetened coconut • slivered almonds.

Jam Swirl Blondies

Makes sixteen 2¼ × 2¼-inch blondies

As we swirled cream cheese into brownie batter for the Marble Cheesecake Brownies, it hit us: Why can't we do the same thing with strawberry jam in a blondie? So here it is, a batter that's thick enough to hold the jam yet thin enough to create a moist, light, crisp blondie. For a sweet treat, ice these with Peanut Butter Icing (page 163).

½ cup strawberry jam

1½ cups all-purpose flour, plus additional for the pan

½ teaspoon baking powder

½ teaspoon salt

8 tablespoons (1 stick) unsalted butter, plus additional for the pan, at room temperature

¾ cup sugar

3 tablespoons heavy cream or whole milk

1 large egg, at room temperature

1 large egg yolk, at room temperature

2 teaspoons vanilla extract

3 ounces semisweet chocolate chips (about ½ cup), or chopped semisweet or bittersweet chocolate

1. Position the rack in the lower third of the oven. Preheat the oven to 350°F. Butter and flour a 9-inch square baking pan; set it aside. In a small saucepan set over low heat, soften the strawberry jam, stirring it constantly for about 3 minutes. Set it aside.

2. In a medium bowl, whisk the flour, baking powder, and salt until well combined. Set aside.

3. In a large bowl, cream the butter and sugar with an electric mixer at medium speed; continue beating until pale yellow and thick, about 4 minutes. Beat in the cream, egg, egg yolk, and vanilla until smooth, about 2 minutes.

4. With a wooden spoon or a rubber spatula, stir in the chocolate chips until well combined; then stir in the flour mixture just until incorporated. Do not beat. Spoon the batter into the prepared pan, spreading it gently to the corners. Dot the strawberry jam across the top of the dough. To swirl the jam through the batter, run a sharp kitchen knife in zigzag patterns over the top without touching the bottom of the pan or lifting the knife up during its course.

5. Bake for 22 minutes, or until the top is light brown and a toothpick or cake tester comes out with a few moist crumbs attached. Set the pan on a wire rack to cool for at least 30 minutes.

6. Cut the blondies into 16 squares while they're still in the pan. Carefully remove them with an offset spatula. Serve immediately, or let cool completely before covering with plastic wrap for storage at room temperature. They will stay fresh for up to 3 days. The blondies can be tightly wrapped in wax paper, sealed in a freezer-safe bag, and frozen for up to 2 months; allow them to thaw at room temperature before serving.

To vary this recipe
Substitute milk chocolate chips • peanut butter chips • or white chocolate chips for the semi-sweet chocolate chips

and/or
Substitute any of the following for the strawberry jam:
apricot jam or preserves • blueberry jam or preserves • boysenberry preserves • fig preserves • gooseberry jam or preserves • grape jam (not jelly) • huckleberry preserves • orange marmalade • peach jam or preserves • pear jam or preserves • raspberry jam or preserves • strawberry-rhubarb jam.

Low-Fat Blondies

Makes sixteen 2¼ × 2¼-inch blondies

Someone once told us they'd canonize us if we could make a moist low-fat blondie. Up to any challenge, we substituted pear butter for most of the fat in the traditional blondie. Pear butter is a thick unsweetened spread, available in many gourmet markets and specialty stores. These chewy, dense blondies are indeed moist and rich, but we're still awaiting word on our saintly status.

1 cup all-purpose flour, plus additional for the pan
1 teaspoon baking powder
½ teaspoon salt
6 tablespoons (¾ stick) unsalted butter, plus additional for the pan, at room temperature
½ cup packed dark brown sugar
½ cup granulated sugar
¼ cup pear butter
2 large eggs, at room temperature
1½ teaspoons vanilla extract
1½ ounces semisweet chocolate chips (about ¼ cup), or chopped semisweet or bittersweet chocolate

1. Position the rack in the lower third of the oven. Preheat the oven to 350°F. Butter and flour a 9-inch square baking pan; set it aside.

2. In a medium bowl, whisk the flour, baking powder, and salt until well combined. Set aside.

3. In a large bowl, cream the butter, dark brown sugar, granulated sugar, and pear butter with an electric mixer at medium speed; continue beating until pale brown and thick, about 4 minutes. Add the eggs one at a time, allowing the first to be thoroughly incorporated before adding the second. After beating in the second egg for 1 minute, beat in the vanilla.

4. With a wooden spoon or a rubber spatula, stir in the flour mixture just until incorporated. Do not beat. Spoon the batter into the prepared pan, spreading it gently to the corners. Sprinkle the chocolate chips over the top.

5. Bake for 22 minutes, or until the top is light brown and a toothpick or cake tester comes out with a few moist crumbs attached. The moment the cake's done, rap it against the oven rack once or twice. Then set it on a wire rack to cool for at least 30 minutes.

6. Cut the blondies into 16 squares while they're still in the pan. Carefully remove them with an offset spatula. Serve immediately, or let cool completely before covering with plastic wrap for storage at room temperature. They will stay fresh for up to 3 days. The blondies can be tightly wrapped in wax paper, sealed in a freezer-safe bag, and frozen for up to 2 months;

allow them to thaw at room temperature before serving.

To vary this recipe

Add one or more of the following spices to the flour mixture:

1½ teaspoons ground cinnamon • 1½ teaspoons ground ginger • ½ teaspoon grated nutmeg

and/or

Substitute one of the following flavorings for the vanilla:

1 teaspoon coconut extract • 1 teaspoon maple extract • 1 teaspoon rum extract • 1 teaspoon almond extract

and/or

Substitute butterscotch chips • mint chocolate chips • peanut butter chips • or white chocolate chips for the semisweet chocolate chips

and/or

Stir in ½ cup of any of the following mix-ins, or ½ cup any combination of the following mix-ins, with the flour mixture:

chopped dried apples • chopped dried apricots • chopped dried pears • chopped pecans • chopped walnuts • cocoa nibs • dried cherries • dried currants • raisins • slivered almonds.

Maple Blondies

Makes sixteen 2¼ × 2¼-inch blondies

In the United States, maple syrup is available in two grades: A (to top pancakes and the like) and B (for baking). To further complicate the matter, Grade A is available in three colors: light amber, medium, and dark. These maple blondies are actually best when made with either a dark amber Grade A or the far more economical Grade B. They taste so much like chocolate chip pancakes, you might be tempted to try them for breakfast.

1¾ cups all-purpose flour, plus additional for the pan

¾ teaspoon baking powder

½ teaspoon salt

12 tablespoons (1½ sticks) unsalted butter, plus additional for the pan, at room temperature

¾ cup packed light brown sugar

½ cup maple syrup

2 large eggs, at room temperature

1½ teaspoons vanilla extract

3 ounces semisweet chocolate chips (about ½ cup), or chopped semisweet or bittersweet chocolate

1. Position the rack in the lower third of the oven. Preheat the oven to 350°F. Butter and flour a 9-inch square baking pan; set it aside.

2. In a medium bowl, whisk the flour, baking powder, and salt until well combined. Set aside.

3. In a large bowl, cream the butter and brown sugar with an electric mixer at medium speed; continue beating until smooth and thick, about 6 minutes. Beat in the maple syrup until uniform; then beat in the eggs one at a time, allowing the first to be thoroughly incorporated before adding the second. Scrape down the sides of the bowl as necessary. After beating in the second egg for 1 minute, beat in the vanilla.

4. With a wooden spoon or a rubber spatula, stir in first the chocolate chips, then the flour mixture, just until incorporated. Do not beat, although the batter will be quite sticky. Spoon the batter into the prepared pan, spreading it gently to the corners.

5. Bake for 35 minutes, or until the top is light brown and a toothpick or cake tester comes out with a few moist crumbs attached. Set the pan on a wire rack to cool for at least 30 minutes.

6. Cut the blondies into 16 squares while they're still in the pan. Carefully remove them with an offset spatula. Serve immediately, or let cool completely before covering with plastic wrap for storage at room temperature. They will stay fresh for up to 3 days. The blondies can be tightly wrapped in wax paper, sealed in a freezer-safe bag, and frozen for up to 3 months; allow them to thaw at room temperature before serving.

To vary this recipe

Add one or more of the following spices to the flour mixture:

1½ teaspoons ground cinnamon • ½ teaspoon grated nutmeg • ½ teaspoon ground cloves • ½ teaspoon ground mace

and/or

Add 1 teaspoon rum extract with the vanilla

and/or

Double the amount of semisweet chocolate chips to 6 ounces

and/or

Substitute butterscotch chips • peanut butter chips • or white chocolate chips for the semisweet chocolate chips

and/or

Stir in ¾ cup of any of the following mix-ins, or ¾ cup any combination of the following mix-ins, with the chocolate chips:

chopped dried apples • chopped pecans • chopped toasted hazelnuts • chopped walnuts • cocoa nibs • dried cranberries • dried currants • raisins • unsalted shelled sunflower seeds.

Marshmallow Blondies

Makes sixteen 2¼ × 2¼-inch blondies

Very sweet, these blondies are also thick and gooey because the marshmallows melt into the batter as it bakes. After baking, the cake will fall as it cools, but it will firm up as well—it needs about 2 hours to come to the right consistency. For a midnight snack extravaganza, these blondies are excellent right out of the freezer.

1¼ cups all-purpose flour, plus additional for the pan

½ teaspoon baking powder

½ teaspoon salt

8 tablespoons (1 stick) unsalted butter, plus additional for the pan, at room temperature

½ cup packed light brown sugar

¼ cup granulated sugar

1 large egg, at room temperature

1 large egg yolk, at room temperature

1½ teaspoons vanilla extract

2 cups mini marshmallows

3 ounces semisweet chocolate chips (about ½ cup), or chopped semisweet or bittersweet chocolate

1. Position the rack in the lower third of the oven. Preheat the oven to 350°F. Butter and flour a 9-inch square baking pan; set it aside.

2. In a medium bowl, whisk the flour, baking powder, and salt until well combined. Set aside.

3. In a large bowl, cream the butter, brown sugar, and granulated sugar with an electric mixer at medium speed; continue beating until pale brown and thick, about 5 minutes. Add the egg and beat until thoroughly incorporated; then beat in the egg yolk and vanilla, scraping down the sides of the bowl as necessary.

4. With a wooden spoon or a rubber spatula, stir in the mini marshmallows and chocolate chips until thoroughly incorporated. Then stir in the flour mixture just until moistened. Do not beat. Spoon the batter into the prepared pan, spreading it gently to the corners.

5. Bake for 22 minutes, or until the top is light brown. The cake will be soft but set, and will firm up as it cools. Set the pan on a wire rack to cool for at least 2 hours.

6. Cut the blondies into 16 squares while they're still in the pan. Carefully remove them with an offset spatula. Serve immediately, or let cool completely before covering with plastic wrap for storage at room temperature. They will stay fresh for up to 2 days. The blondies can be tightly wrapped in wax paper, sealed in a freezer-safe bag, and frozen for up to 2 months; allow them to thaw at room temperature before serving.

To vary this recipe

Add one of the following flavorings with the vanilla:

1 teaspoon almond extract • 1 teaspoon banana extract • 1 teaspoon rum extract

and/or

Substitute butterscotch chips • or peanut butter chips for the semisweet chocolate chips

and/or

Stir in ¾ cup of any of the following mix-ins, or ¾ cup any combination of the following mix-ins, with the chocolate chips:

chopped honey-roasted almonds • chopped plain or honey-roasted peanuts • chopped walnuts • dried blueberries • dried cherries • dried cranberries • slivered almonds • toasted pepitás.

More-Chocolate-Than-Blondie Blondies

Makes twenty-four 2¼ × 2⅛-inch blondies

These thin blondies have just enough dough to hold the chocolate chips together. Cake lovers, be forewarned and look elsewhere. Fudge lovers, take heart: This is perhaps your grail—the most decadent blondie in the book.

1 cup plus 1 tablespoon all-purpose flour, plus additional for the pan
¾ teaspoon baking powder
½ teaspoon salt
10 tablespoons (1 stick plus 2 tablespoons) unsalted butter, plus additional for the pan, at room temperature
1 cup packed light brown sugar
⅓ cup granulated sugar
2 large eggs, at room temperature
1 large egg yolk, at room temperature
2 teaspoons vanilla extract
9 ounces semisweet chocolate chips (about 1½ cups), or chopped semisweet or bittersweet chocolate
9 ounces white chocolate chips (about 1½ cups), or chopped white chocolate

1. Position the rack in the lower third of the oven. Preheat the oven to 350°F. Butter and flour a 9 × 13-inch baking pan; set it aside.

2. In a medium bowl, whisk the flour, baking powder, and salt until well combined. Set aside.

3. In a large bowl, cream the butter, brown sugar, and granulated sugar with an electric mixer at medium speed; continue beating until pale brown and thick, about 6 minutes. Add the eggs one at a time, allowing the first to be thoroughly incorporated before adding the second. Scrape down the sides of the bowl as necessary. Add in the egg yolk and the vanilla, beating for an additional 2 minutes.

4. With a wooden spoon or a rubber spatula, stir in the semisweet and white chocolate chips until well combined. Then stir in the flour mixture just until incorporated. Do not beat. Spoon the batter into the prepared pan, spreading it gently to the corners.

5. Bake for 33 minutes, or until the top is light brown. Because there are so many chips, a toothpick or cake tester will never come out clean. Set the pan on a wire rack to cool for at least 1 hour.

6. Cut the blondies into 24 pieces while they're still in the pan. Carefully remove them with an offset spatula. Serve immediately, or let cool completely before covering with plastic wrap for storage at room temperature. They will stay fresh for up to 4 days. The blondies can be tightly wrapped in wax paper, sealed in a freezer-safe bag, and frozen for up to 3 months; allow them to thaw at room temperature before serving.

To vary this recipe
Add one or more of the following flavorings to the flour mixture:
1 tablespoon finely grated orange zest • 2 teaspoons ground cinnamon • 2 teaspoons ground ginger • 1 teaspoon grated nutmeg
and/or
Substitute one of the following flavorings for the vanilla:
2 teaspoons banana extract • 2 teaspoons maple extract • 2 teaspoons rum extract • 1½ teaspoons almond extract

and/or
Stir in 1 cup of any of the following mix-ins, or 1 cup any combination of the following mix-ins, with the chocolate chips:
chopped pecans • chopped toasted chickpeas • chopped toasted hazelnuts • chopped toasted pepitás • chopped walnuts • pinenuts • plain espresso beans.

Oat Blondies

Makes twenty-four $2\frac{1}{4} \times 2\frac{1}{8}$-inch blondies

Made with rolled oats, these heavy but moist blondies taste like a cross between oatmeal chocolate chip cookies and a dense vanilla pound cake. If you prefer a more toasted taste, bake the oats on a large cookie sheet in a preheated 350°F oven for 5 to 7 minutes, or until browned, tossing them once or twice with a wooden spoon. For a treat, slice the baked blondies open, toast them under a preheated broiler until lightly browned, and serve with vanilla ice cream or raspberry sorbet.

1½ cups all-purpose flour, plus additional for
   the pan
1 teaspoon ground cinnamon
1 teaspoon baking soda
½ teaspoon salt
½ pound (2 sticks) unsalted butter, plus additional
   for the pan, at room temperature
¾ cup granulated sugar
¾ cup packed dark brown sugar
2 large eggs, at room temperature
2 teaspoons vanilla extract
2½ cups rolled oats (not quick-cooking)
6 ounces semisweet chocolate chips (about 1 cup),
   or chopped semisweet or bittersweet chocolate

1. Position the rack in the lower third of the oven. Preheat the oven to 350°F. Butter and flour a 9×13-inch baking pan; set it aside.

2. In a medium bowl, whisk the flour, cinnamon, baking soda, and salt until well combined. Set aside.

3. In a large bowl, cream the butter, granulated sugar, and brown sugar with an electric mixer at medium speed; continue beating until pale brown and thick, about 7 minutes. Add the eggs one at a time, allowing the first to be thoroughly incorporated before adding the second. Scrape down the sides of the bowl as necessary. After beating in the second egg for 1 minute, stir in the vanilla.

4. With a wooden spoon or a rubber spatula, stir in the oats and the chocolate chips until well combined. Then stir in the flour mixture just until incorporated. Do not beat, although the batter will be extremely sticky. Spoon the batter into the prepared pan, pressing it gently into the corners with your fingers.

5. Bake for 30 minutes, or until the top is light brown and a toothpick or cake tester comes out clean. Set the pan on a wire rack to cool for at least 30 minutes.

6. Cut the blondies into 24 pieces while they're still in the pan. Carefully remove them with an offset spatula. Serve immediately, or let cool completely before covering with plastic wrap for storage at room temperature. They will stay fresh for up to 3 days. The blondies can be tightly wrapped in wax paper, sealed in a freezer-safe bag, and frozen for up to 3 months; allow them to thaw at room temperature before serving.

To vary this recipe

Add one or more of the following flavorings with the cinnamon:

2 tablespoons poppy seeds • 1 teaspoon finely grated lemon zest • 1 teaspoon ground ginger • ½ teaspoon grated nutmeg • ½ teaspoon ground cloves

and/or

Add one of the following flavorings with the vanilla:

2 teaspoons maple extract • 1 teaspoon almond extract • 1 teaspoon coconut extract

and/or

Substitute peanut butter chips • or white chocolate chips for the semisweet chocolate chips

and/or

Stir in 1¼ cups of any of the following mix-ins, or 1¼ cups any combination of the following mix-ins, with the chocolate chips:

chopped dried apple • chopped dried pineapple • chopped pecans • chopped toasted hazelnuts • chopped walnuts • cocoa nibs • dried cherries • dried cranberries • dried currants • raisins • Reese's Pieces.

Peanut Butter Blondies

Makes sixteen 2¼ × 2¼-inch blondies

Here's a lunchbox treat guaranteed to satisfy the kid in all of us. With peanut butter, peanut butter chips, brown sugar, and semisweet chocolate chips, these blondies don't need any icing—although Marshmallow Cream Frosting (page 160) can transform them into a cakey version of a Fluffernutter sandwich.

1⅔ cups all-purpose flour, plus additional for the pan

¾ teaspoon baking powder

¼ teaspoon salt

6 tablespoons (¾ stick) unsalted butter, plus additional for the pan, at room temperature

¾ cup granulated sugar

½ cup packed light brown sugar

¼ cup creamy peanut butter

2 large eggs, at room temperature

1 large egg white, at room temperature

2 teaspoons vanilla extract

10 ounces peanut butter chips (one package, about 1½ cups)

3 ounces semisweet chocolate chips (about ½ cup), or chopped semisweet or bittersweet chocolate

1. Position the rack in the lower third of the oven. Preheat the oven to 350°F. Butter and flour a 9-inch square baking pan; set it aside.

2. In a medium bowl, whisk the flour, baking powder, and salt until well combined. Set aside.

3. In a large bowl, cream the butter, granulated sugar, brown sugar, and peanut butter with an electric mixer at medium speed; continue beating until smooth and very thick, about 7 minutes. Add the eggs one at a time, allowing the first to be thoroughly incorporated before adding the second. Scrape down the sides of the bowl as necessary. Beat in the egg white and vanilla until smooth, about 2 minutes.

4. With a wooden spoon or a rubber spatula, stir in the peanut butter chips and the chocolate chips until well combined. Then stir in the flour mixture just until incorporated. Do not beat. Spoon the batter into the prepared pan, spreading it gently to the corners.

5. Bake for 25 minutes, or until the top is light brown and a toothpick or cake tester comes out with a few moist crumbs attached. Set the pan on a wire rack to cool for at least 1 hour.

6. Cut the blondies into 16 squares while they're still in the pan. Carefully remove them with an offset spatula. Serve immediately, or let cool completely before covering with plastic wrap for storage at room temperature. They will stay fresh for up to 3 days. The blondies can be tightly wrapped in wax paper, sealed in a freezer-safe bag, and frozen for up to 3 months; allow them to thaw at room temperature before serving.

To vary this recipe
Add 1 teaspoon banana extract • or 1 teaspoon maple extract with the vanilla
and/or
Substitute white chocolate chips for the semi-sweet chocolate chips

and/or
Stir in ¾ cup of any of the following mix-ins, or ¾ cup any combination of the following mix-ins, with the chocolate chips:
chopped banana chips • chopped honey-roasted almonds • chopped pecans • chopped walnuts • cocoa nibs • dried blueberries • dried strawberries • mini marshmallows • raisins • shredded sweetened coconut • slivered almonds.

Whole Wheat Blondies

Makes twenty-four 2¼ × 2⅛-inch blondies

No, we weren't trying to be healthy when we created these blondies—we wanted to make a firmer, denser blondie. Whole wheat flour and wheat germ indeed make these more toothsome than the some of the others—and, OK, we admit it, a little healthier too. They hold up well to any icing, especially a flavored Buttercream (page 150) or Milk Chocolate Buttercream (page 161). But then so much for being healthy!

1½ cups whole wheat flour
1 teaspoon baking powder
1 teaspoon salt
12 tablespoons (1½ sticks) unsalted butter, plus additional for the pan, at room temperature
1½ cups packed light brown sugar
½ cup granulated sugar
3 large eggs, at room temperature
1 teaspoon vanilla extract
1 teaspoon almond extract
¾ cup wheat germ
6 ounces semisweet chocolate chips (about 1 cup), or chopped semisweet or bittersweet chocolate
1 cup chopped walnuts

1. Position the rack in the lower third of the oven. Preheat the oven to 350°F. Butter a 9 × 13-inch baking pan; set it aside.

2. In a medium bowl, whisk the flour, baking powder, and salt until well combined. Set aside.

3. In a large bowl, cream the butter, brown sugar, and granulated sugar with an electric mixer at medium speed; continue beating until pale brown and thick, about 7 minutes. Add the eggs one at a time, allowing each to be thoroughly incorporated before adding the next. Scrape down the sides of the bowl as necessary. After beating in the third egg for 1 minute, beat in the vanilla and almond extracts.

4. With a wooden spoon or a rubber spatula, stir in the wheat germ, chocolate chips, and walnuts. Then stir in the flour mixture just until incorporated. Do not beat. Spoon the batter into the prepared pan, spreading it gently to the corners.

5. Bake for 30 minutes, or until the top is light brown and a toothpick or cake tester comes out clean. Set the pan on a wire rack to cool for at least 1 hour.

6. Cut the blondies into 24 pieces while they're still in the pan. Carefully remove them with an offset spatula. Serve immediately, or let cool completely before covering with plastic wrap for storage at room temperature. They will stay fresh for up to 3 days. The blondies can be tightly wrapped in wax paper, sealed in a freezer-safe bag, and frozen for up to 3 months; allow them to thaw at room temperature before serving.

To vary this recipe
Add one of the following flavorings to the flour mixture:
2 teaspoons finely grated lemon zest • 2 teaspoons finely grated orange zest • 2 teaspoons ground cinnamon • 2 teaspoons ground ginger

and/or
Substitute butterscotch chips • milk chocolate chips • mint chocolate chips • peanut butter chips • or white chocolate chips for the semisweet chocolate chips
and/or
Stir in 1¼ cups of any of the following mix-ins, or 1¼ cups any combination of the following mix-ins, with the chocolate chips:
chopped banana chips • chopped dried figs • chopped dried mango • dried blueberries • dried cherries • dried cranberries • dried currants • raisins.

Easy Icings, Frostings, and Drizzles

Brown Sugar Icing

Makes about 1½ cups

This very sweet icing tastes somewhat like the butterscotch fudge sold in candy shops across the United States. Since you must "stir down" the hot sugar syrup, use only a heat-safe bowl, such as Pyrex or metal. This icing is best spread on already cut, completely cooled brownies. Like all the other icings given here, this recipe makes enough for a 9 × 13-inch pan of brownies or blondies; if you have leftover icing, either spread it on thicker, or store it covered in the refrigerator for up to 4 days to use on graham crackers, plain cookies, or purchased pound cake.

8 tablespoons (1 stick) unsalted butter, at room temperature
1 cup packed dark brown sugar
¼ cup heavy cream
2 cups confectioners' sugar

1. Melt the butter in a medium saucepan set over low heat. After increasing the heat to medium, stir in the brown sugar with a wooden spoon. Cook, stirring constantly, until the sugar dissolves; simmer for 2 minutes, still stirring constantly. Stir in the cream and bring to a boil.

2. Pour the hot sugar syrup into a large heat-safe bowl and stir until lukewarm. Beat in the confectioners' sugar with an electric mixer at medium speed; continue beating until the frosting is smooth and holds a peak when molded with a spoon. Spread immediately.

To vary this recipe
Beat any of the following flavorings into the finished icing with the confectioners' sugar:
2 teaspoons maple extract • 2 teaspoon rum extract • 2 teaspoons vanilla extract

and/or

Stir ½ cup of any of the following mix-ins into the finished icing:

chopped pecans • chopped toasted chickpeas • chopped toasted hazelnuts • chopped toasted pepitás • chopped walnuts • dried cranberries • raisins • shredded unsweetened coconut.

Buttercream

Makes about 1¼ cups

For the perfect texture, brownies or blondies iced with this classic buttercream need to set up for 20 minutes in the refrigerator. However, they taste best once they come back to room temperature, when the buttercream softens slightly. Buttercream picks up other food odors, so tightly cover the iced brownies.

½ cup plus 1 teaspoon sugar

¼ cup light corn syrup

3 large egg yolks, at room temperature

12 tablespoons (1½ sticks) unsalted butter, at room temperature

1 tablespoon vanilla extract

1. Bring the sugar and corn syrup to a boil in a medium saucepan set over medium heat. Meanwhile, beat the egg yolks lightly in a large bowl.

2. Beat the boiling sugar syrup into the egg yolks in a thin, slow, steady stream, using an electric mixer at medium speed; continue beating until the mixture is cool and pale yellow, about 7 minutes. Beat in the butter 1 tablespoon at a time, scraping down the sides of the bowl as necessary and thoroughly incorporating each tablespoonful before adding the next. Stir in the vanilla. Then spread the frosting immediately on either cut brownies or completely cooled brownies still in the pan. Chill uncut brownies in the refrigerator for 20 minutes before cutting. If icing cut brownies, chill them for 20 minutes after icing.

To vary this recipe

Substitute any of the following flavorings for the vanilla:

1½ tablespoons crème de cassis • 1½ tablespoons bourbon • 1½ tablespoons Cointreau or other orange-flavored liqueur • 1 tablespoon chocolate extract • 2 teaspoons maple extract • 2 teaspoons rum extract • 2 teaspoons strawberry extract • 1½ teaspoons banana extract • 1½ teaspoons orange extract • 1½ teaspoons lemon extract • 1 teaspoon almond extract • 1 teaspoon mint extract

and/or

Stir in ½ cup of any of the following mix-ins, or ½ cup any combination of the following mix-ins, with the vanilla:

chopped Heath bars • chopped honey-roasted almonds • chopped honey-roasted pecans • chopped pecans • chopped toasted hazelnuts • chopped walnuts • crumbled molasses cookies • crumbled Oreo cookies • crumbled pecan sandy cookies • dried currants • M & M's • mint chocolate chips • raisins • Reese's Pieces • semisweet chocolate chips • shredded sweetened coconut • slivered almonds • white chocolate chips.

Chocolate Drizzle

Makes about ½ cup

A drizzle isn't spread on brownies; it is, obviously enough, drizzled on. Use a spoon for thicker lines, a fork for a thin spiderweb design. You can also cut the bottom third off a metal whisk, then dip the whisk in the drizzle and spin it gently over a pan of brownies to create a swirl pattern. A drizzle works best with completely cooled brownies still in the pan.

6 ounces bittersweet or semisweet chocolate, chopped
1 tablespoon solid vegetable shortening

1. Place the chocolate in the top of a double boiler set over simmering water. If you don't have a double boiler, place the chocolate in a heat-safe bowl that fits snugly over a small pot of simmering water. Stir constantly until half the chocolate is melted. Remove the top of the double boiler or the bowl from the pot; then con-tinue stirring, away from the heat, until the chocolate is completely melted. (To melt choco-late in a microwave, see pages 9-10.)

2. Stir the shortening into the warm chocolate; continue stirring until smooth. Set aside to cool for 15 minutes. Drizzle on completely cooled brownies still in the pan; let the pan sit for 1 hour before cutting.

To vary this recipe
Stir in any of the following flavorings with the shortening:
2 teaspoons Chambord or other raspberry-flavored liqueur • 2 teaspoons Cointreau or other orange-flavored liqueur • 1 teaspoon almond extract • 1 teaspoon banana extract • 1 teaspoon vanilla extract • ½ teaspoon mint extract.

Chocolate Fudge Frosting

Makes about 2 cups

Traditionally, an icing is made with confectioners' sugar; a frosting may or may not contain confectioners' sugar. This frosting has no confectioners' sugar at all, so it's very fudgy. Indeed, it has the consistency and texture of fudge. Because it sets up firm, use it the moment it's ready. If it starts to stiffen as you're coating the brownies, simply dip your knife in warm water, then continue.

2 cups sugar
2 tablespoons light corn syrup
⅔ cup heavy cream
3 ounces unsweetened chocolate, chopped
3 tablespoons unsalted butter, at room temperature
1 teaspoon vanilla extract
½ teaspoon salt

1. Combine the sugar, corn syrup, cream, and chocolate in a medium saucepan over medium heat. Stir constantly until the sugar dissolves and the mixture bubbles, then clip a candy thermometer to the inside of the pan. Cook without stirring until the mixture reaches 240°F (soft-ball stage).

2. Pour the boiling mixture into a large heat-safe bowl and add the butter. Do not stir, but allow the butter to melt completely. When the outside of the bowl feels lukewarm to the touch, beat in the vanilla and salt with an electric mixer at medium speed. Beat only until the mixture is spreadable and holds its shape when molded with a spoon, about 1 minute. Do not overmix, or the mixture will turn to fudge. Spread immediately.

To vary this recipe
Substitute any of the following flavorings for the vanilla:
1½ tablespoons Amaretto or other almond-flavored liqueur • 1½ tablespoons Cointreau or other orange-flavored liqueur • 1½ tablespoons Frangelico or other hazelnut-flavored liqueur • 2 teaspoons almond extract • 2 teaspoons rum extract • 1 teaspoon mint extract
and/or
Stir ¾ cup of any of the following mix-ins, or ¾ cup any combination of the following mix-ins, into the finished frosting:
chopped Heath bars • chopped pecans • chopped toasted hazelnuts • chopped walnuts • mini marshmallows • raisins • Reese's Pieces • white chocolate chips.

Cocoa Frosting

Makes about 1¼ cups

This is a simpler, uncooked version of Chocolate Fudge Frosting (page 152). Halfway between a buttercream and a chocolate icing, this easy frosting makes a great topping for almost any brownie or blondie in this book. It sets up fast, so use it the moment it's ready.

4 tablespoons (½ stick) unsalted butter, at room temperature

¼ cup plus 2 tablespoons unsweetened cocoa powder, sifted

3 tablespoons heavy cream

1 tablespoon light corn syrup

2 teaspoons vanilla extract

1½ cups confectioners' sugar

1. In a large bowl, beat the butter, cocoa powder, cream, corn syrup, and vanilla with an electric mixer at medium speed; continue beating until smooth and thick, about 4 minutes, scraping down the sides of the bowl as necessary.

2. Beat in the sugar, ½ cup at a time, letting each addition be fully incorporated before adding the next. Beat an additional minute once all the sugar is incorporated; spread immediately.

To vary this recipe

Substitute any of the following flavorings for the vanilla:

1 tablespoon crème de cassis • 1 tablespoon Cointreau or other orange-flavored liqueur • 1 tablespoon Frangelico or other hazelnut-flavored liqueur • 2 teaspoons maple extract • 1½ teaspoons rum extract • 1 teaspoon almond extract • 1 teaspoon mint extract • 1 teaspoon orange extract

and/or

Stir ½ cup of any of the following mix-ins, or ½ cup any combination of the following mix-ins, into the finished frosting:

chopped honey-roasted peanuts • chopped pecans • chopped toasted hazelnuts • chopped toasted pepitás • chopped walnuts • cocoa nibs • Raisinets • raisins • Reese's Pieces • slivered almonds • unsalted shelled sunflower seeds.

Cola Icing

Makes about 4½ cups

Designed primarily to go with Cola Brownies (page 50), this traditional Southern frosting is very rich—so rich, in fact, that we added pecans to the base recipe for a crunchy texture that balances the thick sweetness. Toast chopped pecans on a cookie sheet in a 350°F oven for 7 to 9 minutes, tossing them occasionally with a wooden spoon. This sweet icing goes well with any cakey brownie.

8 tablespoons (1 stick) unsalted butter, at room temperature, cut into 1-tablespoon pieces
3 tablespoons unsweetened cocoa powder, sifted
⅓ cup carbonated cola
4 cups confectioners' sugar
1 cup chopped pecans, toasted

1. In a large bowl, beat the butter, cocoa powder, and cola with an electric mixer set at medium speed; continue beating until smooth, scraping down the sides of the bowl as necessary.

2. Slowly add the confectioners' sugar, 1 cup at a time, beating each addition until thoroughly incorporated before adding the next. Stir in the pecans; spread immediately.

In the South, the traditional variation would be to stir 1 cup mini marshmallows into the icing with the pecans.

Cream Cheese Frosting

Makes about 1¼ cups

Because of various factors (the day's humidity, the fat content of the cream cheese, the temperature of the cream cheese itself), this recipe for a classic, creamy frosting calls for a range of confectioners' sugar. Remember that the confectioners' sugar continues to thicken the frosting as it sits—stop adding the sugar when the icing has just thickened but is still spreadable.

4 ounces cream cheese (regular or low-fat, but not fat-free), at room temperature

4 tablespoons (½ stick) unsalted butter, at room temperature

1 teaspoon vanilla extract

1½ to 2 cups confectioners' sugar

Beat the cream cheese, butter, and vanilla in a large bowl with an electric mixer on medium speed; continue beating until smooth and light, about 2 minutes. Beat in the confectioners' sugar, ½ cup at a time, scraping down the sides of the bowl as necessary. Add only enough confectioners' sugar to make a spreadable icing with a slightly stiff consistency. Let sit for 15 minutes before spreading.

To vary this recipe
Substitute any of the following flavorings for the vanilla:

1 tablespoon grated lemon zest • 1 tablespoon chocolate extract • 1 tablespoon poppy seeds • 1½ teaspoons strawberry extract • 1 teaspoon almond extract • 1 teaspoon lemon extract • 1 teaspoon maple extract • 1 teaspoon mint extract • 1 teaspoon orange extract • 1 teaspoon raspberry extract • 1 teaspoon rum extract

and/or

Stir ½ cup of any of the following nuts into the finished frosting:

chopped pecans • chopped toasted hazelnuts • chopped walnuts • slivered almonds • toasted pinenuts.

Five Minute Chocolate Frosting

Makes 1½ cups

This frosting is thick, fudgy, and chewy—and it's a lot easier to make than more traditional chocolate frostings, thanks to the sweetened condensed milk. It sets up very fast and is quite thick, so it's best spread on cut brownies with a spatula, using the same technique as you would if you were painting with a palette knife.

2 ounces unsweetened chocolate, chopped
One 14-ounce can sweetened condensed milk (regular, low-fat, or fat-free)
1 tablespoon vanilla extract
Additional milk (whole, low-fat, or fat-free) as necessary

1. Place the chocolate in the top of a double boiler set over simmering water. If you don't have a double boiler, place the chocolate in a heat-safe bowl that fits snugly over a small pot of simmering water. Stir constantly until melted; then stir in the sweetened condensed milk. Raise the heat to high to boil the water rapidly in the pot below. Cook, stirring constantly, until the mixture is very thick, about 5 minutes.

2. Remove from the heat and stir in the vanilla. Cool slightly before using. The mixture continues to thicken as it cools; to keep the frosting pliable, stir in milk in 1 teaspoon amounts as necessary while spreading.

To vary this recipe
Substitute any of the following flavorings for the vanilla:
1 tablespoon Frangelico or other hazelnut-flavored liqueur • 2 teaspoons almond extract • 2 teaspoons orange extract • 2 teaspoons rum extract • 1½ teaspoons raspberry extract.

Ganache Icing

Makes about 1½ cups

A decadent icing, this is basically a spreadable chocolate truffle. For a treat, spread this thin candy-like icing on the tops and sides of cut brownies, cool them completely, then freeze for 24 hours, wrapped tightly in wax paper. They turn into frozen candy bars.

6 ounces bittersweet or semisweet chocolate, chopped
½ cup heavy cream
1 teaspoon vanilla extract

1. Place the chocolate and cream in the top of a double boiler set over simmering water. If you don't have a double boiler, place the chocolate and cream in a heat-safe bowl that fits snugly over a small pot of simmering water. Stir constantly until half the chocolate is melted. Remove the top of the double boiler or the bowl from the pot; then continue stirring, away from the heat, until all the chocolate is melted. (To melt chocolate in a microwave, see pages 9-10.) Transfer the mixture to a large bowl and stir until smooth and cool. Stir in the vanilla and refrigerate for 20 minutes.

2. Once the mixture is like a paste, beat it with an electric mixer at high speed for 2 minutes, until smooth and creamy. Spread immediately either on cut brownies or on completely cooled brownies still in the pan. Chill the pan in the refrigerator for 20 minutes before cutting.

To vary this recipe
Substitute any of the following flavorings for the vanilla:
1 teaspoon almond extract • 1 teaspoon orange extract • 1 teaspoon maple extract • 1 teaspoon raspberry extract • 1 teaspoon rum extract • 1 teaspoon strawberry extract • ½ teaspoon mint extract.

Grasshopper Frosting

Makes about 1½ cups

This minty, refreshing frosting is even better the second day, after the flavors have melded. Store the frosted brownies tightly covered, either in the refrigerator or at room temperature.

½ cup Marshmallow Fluff or other marshmallow creme
6 tablespoons (¾ stick) unsalted butter, at room temperature
2 tablespoons crème de menthe liqueur
½ teaspoon mint extract (optional)
2 cups confectioners' sugar, or more as necessary
½ cup finely chopped bittersweet chocolate or mini semisweet chocolate chips

1. In a large bowl, cream the Marshmallow Fluff and butter with an electric mixer at medium speed until smooth and uniform. Beat in the crème de menthe and the mint extract, if desired.

2. Beat in the confectioners' sugar in ½-cup increments, making sure each addition is incorporated before adding the next and adding more confectioners' sugar if necessary to achieve a spreadable consistency. Stir in the chocolate chips; spread immediately on cooled brownies or blondies still in the pan.

To vary this recipe
Substitute milk chocolate chips • or white chocolate chips for the bittersweet chips
and/or
Stir in ½ cup of any of the following mix-ins, or ½ cup any combination of the following mix-ins, with the chocolate chips:
chopped pecans • chopped toasted hazelnuts • chopped toasted pepitás • chopped walnuts • cocoa nibs • Reese's Pieces • slivered almonds.

Lemon Curd

Makes about 1½ cups

This easy lemon curd uses less butter than most, so it's more spreadable. It's best used as a thin glaze on already cut brownies. For an elegant dessert, place a small dollop of lemon curd on a plate, set a brownie on it, then garnish with whipped cream.

3 large eggs, at room temperature
1½ cups sugar
1 tablespoon finely grated lemon zest
¾ cup lemon juice
3 tablespoons unsalted butter, at room
  temperature

Combine the eggs, sugar, lemon zest, lemon juice, and butter in the top of a double boiler set over simmering water. If you don't have a dou-ble boiler, place all the ingredients in a heat-safe bowl that fits snugly over a small pot of simmer-ing water. Whisk constantly until thick, glossy, and smooth, about 12 minutes. Cool to room temperature before spreading.

You can also make other citrus curds:
- Grapefruit Curd: use finely grated grapefruit zest and grapefruit juice
- Key Lime Curd: use finely grated Key lime zest and Key lime juice
- Lime Curd: use finely grated lime zest and lime juice
- Orange Curd: use finely grated orange zest and orange juice
- Tangerine Curd: use finely grated tangerine zest and tangerine juice

Marshmallow Cream Frosting

Makes about 2 cups

Marshmallow Fluff or Marshmallow Creme? The choice depends on which side of the Mississippi River you live on. Either way, this frosting is like spreadable marshmallows: sweet, light, and sticky. It needs to cool for about 30 minutes before it reaches the right consistency to spread on already cut brownies.

8 tablespoons (1 stick) unsalted butter, at room temperature
1⅓ cups Marshmallow Fluff or other marshmallow creme
1 teaspoon vanilla extract
2 cups confectioners' sugar, sifted

Melt the butter in a medium saucepan set over medium heat. Stir in the Marshmallow Fluff; continue to cook and stir just until the fluff has melted and the mixture is smooth. Remove from the heat; stir in the vanilla, then the confectioners' sugar. Continue stirring until the sugar has dissolved and the mixture is uniform. Allow to cool for 30 minutes, or until a spreadable consistency is reached. Spread onto cut brownies.

To vary this recipe
Substitute any of the following flavorings for the vanilla:
1 teaspoon banana extract • 1 teaspoon coconut extract • 1 teaspoon maple extract • 1 teaspoon rum extract
and/or
Stir ½ cup of any of the following into the finished frosting:
butterscotch chips • chopped Heath bars • cocoa nibs • miniature semisweet chocolate chips • peanut butter chips • Reese's Pieces • shredded sweetened coconut.

Milk Chocolate Buttercream

Makes about 1½ cups

This extremely rich buttercream is made by melting milk chocolate, then adding enough butter to reset the chocolate into a frosting. A little goes a long way, but it's still the ultimate decadence.

9 ounces milk chocolate, chopped
3 ounces bittersweet or semisweet chocolate, chopped
12 tablespoons (1½ sticks) unsalted butter, at room temperature
1 teaspoon vanilla extract

1. Place both chocolates in the top of a double boiler set over simmering water. If you don't have a double boiler, place both chocolates in a heat-safe bowl that fits snugly over a small pot of simmering water. Stir constantly until half the chocolate is melted. Remove the top of the double boiler or the bowl from the pot; then continue stirring, away from the heat, until the chocolate is completely melted. (To melt chocolate in a microwave, see pages 9-10.)

2. In a large bowl, beat the butter until smooth, light, and pale yellow, about 2 minutes. Slowly pour the melted chocolate in a thin, slow, steady stream into the beaten butter; continue beating until thick and smooth, about 3 minutes. Then stir in the vanilla. Spread immediately either on cut brownies or on completely cooled brownies still in the pan.

To vary this recipe
Stir ½ cup of any of the following into the finished buttercream:
chopped honey-roasted almonds • chopped pecans • chopped toasted chickpeas • chopped toasted hazelnuts • chopped toasted pepitás • chopped unsalted peanuts • chopped walnuts • slivered almonds • toasted pinenuts.

Mocha Cream Frosting

Makes about 1½ cups

For this frosting, a food processor whips the cream to just the right consistency, neither too airy nor too thick. But be very careful—overprocessing the cream produces butter. Crush the instant coffee using a mortar and pestle, or between two sheets of wax paper with the bottom of a large, heavy pot. For the best results, spread this frosting onto precut brownies.

3 tablespoons confectioners' sugar
2 tablespoons unsweetened cocoa powder
1 tablespoon instant coffee powder, crushed
1 cup heavy cream

Sift the sugar, cocoa powder, and instant coffee together into the bowl of a food processor; pour in the cream. Process just until thick and smooth, scraping down the sides of the bowl as necessary. Spread the mixture onto cut brownies.

To vary this recipe
Stir ⅓ cup of any of the following into the finished frosting with a wooden spoon:
chopped 100 Grand bars • chopped Baby Ruth bars • chopped Butterfinger bars • chopped Heath bars • chopped PayDay bars • chopped pecans • chopped toasted hazelnuts • chopped walnuts • cocoa nibs • crushed biscotti • M & M's • Raisinets • Reese's Pieces.

Peanut Butter Icing

Makes about 1¼ cups

This simple icing is so thick, it's best spread on already-cut brownies. It's terrific on Banana Brownies (page 14), but its salty taste also works well against any of the sweeter brownies like White Chocolate Brownies (page 106) or Marzipan Brownies (page 78). Any extra icing is great on plain graham crackers.

1 cup smooth peanut butter (not natural or organic)
6 tablespoons confectioners' sugar
½ teaspoon vanilla extract

In a large bowl, stir the peanut butter, confectioners' sugar, and vanilla with a wooden spoon until smooth. Spread immediately.

To vary this recipe

Substitute any of the following flavorings for the vanilla:

½ teaspoon banana extract • ½ teaspoon maple extract • ½ teaspoon strawberry extract
and/or
Stir ⅓ cup of any of the following into the finished icing:

chopped banana chips • chopped honey-roasted or unsalted peanuts • cocoa nibs • dried strawberries • raisins • slivered almonds.

Seven Minute Frosting

Makes about 2 cups

Once, Seven Minute Frosting ruled the day, a favorite of '50s housewives. It's a shame it's now out of vogue. It tastes like a light marshmallow cream and works well on any brownie or blondie—provided your kids don't get to the bowl first.

2 large egg whites, at room temperature
2 tablespoons water
¾ cup sugar
½ teaspoon cream of tartar
¼ teaspoon salt
1 teaspoon vanilla extract

1. Beat the egg whites, water, sugar, cream of tartar, and salt in the top of a double boiler (off the heat) or in a heat-safe bowl, using an electric mixer at medium speed, until the mixture is smooth and uniform.

2. Set the top of the double boiler over simmering water, or place the heat-safe bowl snugly over a small pot of simmering water. Continue beating until the frosting is thick and dense, about 7 minutes. Remove the top of the double boiler or the bowl from the pot, and stir in the vanilla. Spread immediately.

To vary this recipe
Stir in ½ cup of any of the following with the vanilla:
chopped Heath bars • chopped pecans • chopped Snickers bars • chopped walnuts • cocoa nibs • M & M's • miniature semisweet chocolate chips • Reese's Pieces • shredded sweetened coconut.

Sour Cream Icing

Makes about 1½ cups

For this tangy icing, the sour cream should be at room temperature. If it is not, the chocolate may seize and the icing will be useless, for you can't reheat the sour cream without its breaking. This icing is the perfect foil to some of the sweeter treats in this book, like Malt Brownies (page 70) or Coconut Blondies (page 120).

6 ounces bittersweet or semisweet chocolate, chopped
8 ounces sour cream (regular, low-fat, or fat-free), at room temperature
1 teaspoon vanilla extract

1. Place the chocolate in the top of a double boiler set over simmering water. If you don't have a double boiler, place the chocolate in a heat-safe bowl that fits snugly over a small pot of simmering water. Stir constantly until half the chocolate is melted. Remove the top of the double boiler or the bowl from the pot; then continue stirring, away from the heat, until the chocolate is completely melted. (To melt chocolate in a microwave, see pages 9-10.)

2. Beat in the sour cream and vanilla with an electric mixer on low speed. Continue beating until the frosting can hold a peak when molded with a spoon, about 4 minutes. Spread immediately.

To vary this recipe
Substitute any of the following flavorings for the vanilla:
1 teaspoon almond extract • 1 teaspoon mint extract • 1 teaspoon raspberry extract • 1 teaspoon rum extract
and/or
Stir in ½ cup of any of the following mix-ins, or ½ cup any combination of the following mix-ins with the vanilla:
chopped banana chips • chopped pecans • chopped toasted hazelnuts • chopped walnuts • cocoa nibs • dried cherries • dried cranberries • mini semisweet chocolate chips • toasted pinenuts

Vanilla Icing

Makes about 1½ cups

This very simple icing can also be used as a drizzle: Simply swirl it onto a pan of brownies, using a spoon for wide ribbons or a fork for thinner ones. It can make a beautiful spiderweb pattern over More-Chocolate-Than-Blondie Blondies (page 140).

2 cups confectioners' sugar
1 tablespoon plus 2 teaspoons milk (whole, 2%, 1%, or fat-free), plus more if necessary
2 teaspoons vanilla extract

Stir the sugar, milk, and vanilla in a large bowl until smooth and uniform. Add more milk, 1 teaspoon at a time, if the icing is too stiff. Spread immediately either on cut brownies or on completely cooled brownies still in the pan. Set aside for 1 hour, or until the icing is set.

To vary this recipe
Substitute any of the following flavorings for the vanilla:
2 teaspoons Amaretto or other almond-flavored liqueur • 2 teaspoons bourbon • 2 teaspoons crème de cassis • 2 teaspoons Cointreau or other orange-flavored liqueur • 2 teaspoons Frangelico or other hazelnut-flavored liqueur • 2 teaspoons maple extract • 1½ teaspoons rum extract • 1 teaspoon lemon extract
or
Substitute orange juice for the milk.

Fun with Brownie Mixes

Brownie Mix Baked Alaska

Makes 12 servings

Baked Alaska was once the essence of style: hot and cold, a baked meringue shell with cold ice cream inside. To make this dessert, harden the ice cream by first scooping out twelve balls, placing them on a cookie sheet, and freezing them overnight. They'll then be hard enough to withstand the high temperature in the oven. You needn't, of course, make twelve desserts—make as many as you want, setting aside the leftover brownies and cutting the meringue recipe in half or even thirds.

FOR THE BROWNIES
Unsalted butter for the pan
All-purpose flour for the pan
One 19.9-ounce package brownie mix, or
  any brownie mix suitable for a 9 × 13-inch
  baking pan
3 large eggs, at room temperature,
  lightly beaten
8 tablespoons (1 stick) unsalted butter, melted,
¼ cup milk (whole, low-fat, or fat-free)

FOR THE MERINGUE
6 large egg whites, at room temperature
1½ cups sugar
3 tablespoons water

FOR THE ICE CREAM
Twelve ½-cup scoops chocolate ice cream,
  frozen very hard

1. Position the rack in the lower third of the oven. Preheat the oven to 350°F. Butter and flour a 9 × 13-inch baking pan; set it aside.

2. Place the brownie mix, beaten eggs, melted butter, and milk in a large bowl; stir with a wooden spoon until smooth, then pour into the prepared pan. Bake for 30 minutes, or until a toothpick or cake tester comes out clean. Cool the pan on a wire rack for 30 minutes; then cut into twelve 3 × 3¼-inch brownies. These first two steps can be done up to 2 days in advance; cover the brownies with plastic wrap and store at room temperature.

3. Preheat the oven to 500°F.

4. To make the meringue, beat the egg whites in a large bowl with a mixer at high speed until soft peaks form, about 5 minutes. Set aside. Combine the sugar and water in a small saucepan set over medium heat; stir constantly until the sugar dissolves. Raise the heat to high and boil for 2 minutes without stirring. Remove the sugar syrup from the heat and pour it in a slow, thin, steady stream into the egg whites, beating all the while with an electric mixer at high speed. Continue beating for 5 minutes, or until cool.

5. Place the cut brownies on two large cookie sheets, spacing them about 2 inches apart. Place 1 scoop of chocolate ice cream on top of each brownie. Cover each scoop with meringue, spreading it to the edges of the brownie and sealing it by gently pressing down with a rubber spatula. The meringue should be at least ¼ inch thick at all points.

6. Bake in the oven until the meringue is lightly browned, about 5 minutes. Serve immediately.

To vary this recipe
You can use any brownie recipe in this book—try Bourbon Brownies (page 18) or Cocoa Nib Brownies (page 44) for unusual variations.
and/or
Replace the chocolate ice cream with butterscotch ice cream • chocolate chip ice cream • cookie dough ice cream • peach ice cream • rocky road ice cream • strawberry ice cream • or vanilla ice cream
and/or
Use one of the blondie recipes in this book, rather than a brownie mix or recipe
and/or
Spoon 2 teaspoons butterscotch syrup • or chocolate syrup over the brownie before topping with ice cream
and/or
Sprinkle the meringue with finely chopped nuts • or chocolate sprinkles before baking.

Brownie Mix Black Forest Cake

Makes 12 servings

Long a staple in German restaurants across the country, a classic Black Forest Cake is a chocolate cake with layers of whipped cream and cherries. We can think of no simpler way to make this pretty dessert than with a brownie mix. Confectioners' sugar stabilizes the whipped cream—it won't weep, so you can make the cake in advance, storing it covered in the refrigerator.

FOR THE CAKE

Unsalted butter and all-purpose flour for the pans

One 19.9-ounce package brownie mix, or any brownie mix suitable for a 9 × 13-inch baking pan

3 large egg yolks, at room temperature, lightly beaten

8 tablespoons (1 stick) unsalted butter, melted

¼ cup milk (whole, low-fat, or fat-free)

3 large egg whites, at room temperature, beaten until soft peaks form

FOR THE FILLING

1 cup heavy cream

2 tablespoons confectioners' sugar

One 21-ounce can cherry pie filling

1. Position the rack in the lower third of the oven. Preheat the oven to 350°F. Butter and flour two 8-inch round cake pans; set them aside.

2. Place the brownie mix, beaten egg yolks, melted butter, and milk in a large bowl; beat with a wooden spoon until smooth. Then gently fold in the beaten egg whites just until incorporated.

Pour into the prepared cake pans. Bake for 20 minutes, or until a toothpick or cake tester comes out clean. Cool the pans on a wire rack for 10 minutes; then unmold the cakes and cool to room temperature on a wire rack, about 1 hour.

3. Beat the cream and confectioners' sugar in a large bowl, using an electric mixer at high speed, until soft but firm peaks form, about 3 minutes.

4. Place one cake round on a cake plate; mound half the whipped cream around the edges, making a rim; then fill the center with half the cherry pie filling. Place the second cake round on top and repeat with the remaining cream and pie filling. Serve immediately, or cover the cake loosely in plastic wrap and store in the refrigerator for up to 3 days. Allow it to come back to room temperature before serving.

To vary this recipe

Stir ½ cup of any of the following into the brownie batter with the milk:

chopped pecans • chopped walnuts • dried cherries • dried cranberries • dried strawberries • raisins • sliced almonds

and/or

Substitute any of the following for the cherry pie filling:

canned apple pie filling • blackberry pie filling • blueberry pie filling • peach pie filling.

Brownie Mix Bourbon Balls

Makes about 48 balls

Years ago, bourbon balls were the one vice allowed Southern Baptist grandmothers. Sure, these candy-dish treats no longer carry the patina of sin, but they're still decadent enough to be one of the most pleasant vices around—and with a brownie mix, they're easy to make.

Unsalted butter for the pan
All-purpose flour for the pan
One 19.9-ounce package brownie mix, or any brownie mix suitable for a 9 × 13-inch baking pan
3 large eggs, at room temperature, lightly beaten
8 tablespoons (1 stick) unsalted butter, melted
¼ cup milk (whole, low-fat, or fat-free)
¼ cup bourbon, or more as needed
3 cups finely chopped pecans

1. Position the rack in the lower third of the oven. Preheat the oven to 350°F. Butter and flour a 9 × 13-inch baking pan; set it aside.

2. Place the brownie mix, beaten eggs, melted butter, and milk in a large bowl; stir with a wooden spoon until smooth, then pour into the prepared pan. Bake for 30 minutes, or until a toothpick or cake tester comes out clean. Cool the pan on a wire rack for at least 3 hours, or preferably uncovered overnight, so the cake can dry out a bit.

3. Crumble the baked brownies from the pan into the bowl of a food processor. Add the bourbon and pulse the machine until a soft dough is formed. If necessary, add more bourbon through the feed tube, 1 teaspoon at a time. But take care: The dough must not be too wet; it should have a fudge-like consistency.

4. Spread the chopped pecans out on a large piece of wax paper. Roll 1-inch balls of the dough between your palms, then roll them in the nuts. Refrigerate, covered, for at least 1 hour before serving. Store covered in the refrigerator for up to 1 week.

To vary this recipe
This recipe can be made with Lunchbox Brownies (page 68), Cake Brownies, (page 34, or Whole Wheat Blondies (page 146). Or use a more exotic brownie recipe and begin at step 3 with such brownies as Brown Sugar Brownies (page 20); Buttermilk Brownies (page 30); Coffee Brownies (page 48) for Irish Coffee balls; Cola Brownies (page 50) for bourbon-and-cola balls
and/or
Substitute Kahlúa or other coffee-flavored liqueur • rum • or whiskey for the bourbon
and/or
Substitute chopped walnuts • cocoa nibs • or shredded sweetened coconut for the pecans.

Brownie Mix Bundt Cake

Makes about 8 servings

The Bundt pan was designed by a group of women in Minneapolis who were members of Hadassah. They wanted a light version of the cast-iron pan used to make kugelhupf. Nordic Products made a few for them, and sold a few to the public—but nothing really happened until the 1966 Pillsbury Bake-Off featured a fudge cake in a Bundt pan as one of its finalists. From that moment on, the Bundt pan has been an American staple. Here's a simple Bundt chocolate fudge cake that's perfect for holiday get-togethers, family reunions, or last-minute drop-by company. Serve it with sweetened whipped cream, purchased ice cream, or Lemon Curd (page 159).

Unsalted butter for the pan
All-purpose flour for the pan
One 19.9-ounce package brownie mix, or any brownie mix suitable for a 9 × 13-inch baking pan
One 3.9-ounce package instant chocolate pudding
4 large eggs, at room temperature, lightly beaten
8 tablespoons (1 stick) unsalted butter, melted
1 cup sour cream (regular, low-fat, or fat-free)

1. Position the rack in the lower third of the oven. Preheat the oven to 350°F. Butter and flour a 12-cup Bundt cake pan; set it aside.

2. Place the brownie mix, instant pudding mix, beaten eggs, melted butter, and sour cream in a large bowl; stir with a wooden spoon until smooth, then pour into the prepared pan.

3. Bake for 45 minutes or until a toothpick or cake tester comes out with a few moist crumbs attached. Cool the pan on a wire rack for 30 minutes; then unmold the cake, invert it, and cool completely on a wire rack. Serve immediately, or cover in plastic wrap and store at room temperature. The cake will stay fresh for up to 4 days. It can also be tightly wrapped in wax paper, sealed in a plastic wrap, and frozen for up to 2 months; allow the cake to thaw at room temperature before serving.

To vary this recipe
Add one of the following flavorings to the batter with the sour cream:
1 tablespoon vanilla extract • 2 teaspoons rum extract • 2 teaspoons maple extract • 1½ teaspoons almond extract • 1½ teaspoons anise extract • 1 teaspoon peppermint extract
and/or
Stir ¾ cup of one of the following into the batter with the sour cream:
almond M & M's • chopped honey-roasted peanuts • chopped pecans • chopped walnuts • cocoa nibs • pinenuts • shredded sweetened coconut • white chocolate chips.

Brownie Mix Cookies

Makes about 36 cookies

These easy cookies taste like brownies, but they are crisper and more delicate. What's more, the extra surface area exposed during baking heats the chocolate in the mix more intensely than would happen in a baking pan—so the cookies have a deeper, more sophisticated, slightly bitter taste. They're great for ice cream sandwiches.

Unsalted butter for the cookie sheet
1 large egg, at room temperature
1 large egg white, at room temperature
One 19.9-ounce package brownie mix, or any
  brownie mix suitable for a 9 × 13-inch baking pan
6 tablespoons (¾ stick) unsalted butter, at room
  temperature
3 ounces bittersweet or semisweet chocolate chips
  (about ½ cup)
½ cup chopped walnuts

1. Position two racks in the oven, one in the upper third and one in the lower third. Preheat the oven to 350°F. Butter two large cookie sheets; set them aside.

2. Beat the egg and egg white together in a large bowl until frothy. Add the brownie mix, and melted butter; stir with a wooden spoon until smooth. Stir in the chocolate chips and chopped walnuts. Drop level tablespoonsful of the batter onto the prepared cookie sheets, spacing the cookies 2 inches apart. If there's extra batter, reserve it for a second baking, once the cookie sheets have cooled.

3. Place one cookie sheet on each oven rack; and bake for 5 minutes; then reverse the sheets and bake for an additional 6 minutes. Remove the sheets from the oven and allow them to cool on wire racks for 5 minutes; then transfer the cookies from the sheets to the wire racks with a spatula, and allow them to cool completely. Store the cookies, covered and at room temperature, for up to 4 days. They can also be wrapped tightly in plastic wrap, then placed in a freezer-safe bag and frozen for up to 2 months; thaw completely before serving.

To vary this recipe
Stir any of the following flavorings into the batter with the chocolate chips:
1 tablespoon vanilla extract • 2 teaspoons rum extract • 2 teaspoons maple extract • 1½ teaspoons almond extract • 1 teaspoon peppermint extract
and/or
Substitute milk chocolate chips • mint chocolate chips • or white chocolate chips for the bittersweet chips
and/or
Substitute chopped pecans • chopped toasted hazelnuts • or raisins for the walnuts.

Brownie Mix Heath Bar Crunch Squares

Makes sixteen 2¼ × 2¼-inch brownies

These luscious treats are simply two layers of brownie-mix batter enclosing crushed Heath bars. What could possibly be better—or easier? Check out the variations for other candy ideas.

Unsalted butter for the pan
All-purpose flour for the pan
One 19.9-ounce package brownie mix, or any brownie mix suitable for a 9 × 13-inch baking pan
3 large eggs, at room temperature, lightly beaten
8 tablespoons (1 stick) unsalted butter, melted
¼ cup milk (whole, low-fat, or fat-free)
Three 1.4-ounce Heath bars, chopped into ½-inch pieces

1. Position the rack in the lower third of the oven. Preheat the oven to 350°F. Butter and flour a 9-inch square baking pan; set it aside.

2. Place the brownie mix, beaten eggs, melted butter, and milk in a large bowl; stir with a wooden spoon until smooth. Pour half the batter into the prepared pan, spreading it gently to the corners. Sprinkle the chopped Heath bars evenly over the top. Then drop the remaining batter by tablespoonsful onto the candy and batter, creating a second layer without having to spread it.

3. Bake for 40 minutes or until a toothpick or cake tester comes out with a few moist crumbs attached. Check the cake in a few places since the candy may stick to the toothpick or tester. Set the pan on a wire rack to cool completely.

4. Cut the brownies into 16 squares while they're still in the pan. Carefully remove them with an offset spatula. Serve immediately, or cover with plastic wrap for storage at room temperature. They will stay fresh for up to 3 days. Because of the melted Heath bars, these brownies do not freeze well.

To vary this recipe
Substitute ¼ cup of any of the following for the milk:
Baileys Original Irish Cream • Frangelico or other hazelnut-flavored liqueur • gold rum • half-and-half • heavy cream • Kahlúa or other coffee-flavored liqueur
and/or
Stir any of the following into the batter with the milk:
1 tablespoon vanilla extract • 2 teaspoons ground cinnamon • 2 teaspoons ground ginger • 1 teaspoon almond extract • ½ teaspoon ground mace • ½ teaspoon grated nutmeg
and/or
Substitute any of the following for the Heath bars:
1 cup chopped candied walnuts • 1 cup chopped Butterfinger bars • 1 cup crushed hard peppermint candies • 1 cup crushed peanut brittle.

Brownie Mix Ice Cream Cake

Makes 12 servings

A great idea for anyone's birthday, this fun cake will please all the kids in your life. A brownie mix and purchased ice cream make it a snap. You can also make the cake up to a month in advance, storing it tightly covered in the freezer. Once the ice cream melts, however, the cake cannot be refrozen.

Unsalted butter for the pan
All-purpose flour for the pan
2 large eggs, at room temperature
1 large egg yolk, at room temperature
One 19.9-ounce package brownie mix, or any
   brownie mix suitable for a 9 × 13-inch
   baking pan
8 tablespoons (1 stick) unsalted butter, melted
¼ cup strong coffee, at room temperature
1 pint coffee ice cream, softened
1 pint chocolate ice cream, softened

1. Position the rack in the lower third of the oven. Preheat the oven to 350°F. Butter and flour a 9 × 13-inch baking pan; set it aside.

2. Beat the eggs and egg yolk lightly in a large bowl. Add the brownie mix, melted butter, and coffee; stir with a wooden spoon until smooth. Pour the batter into the prepared pan, spreading it gently to the corners.

3. Bake for 30 minutes, or until a toothpick or cake tester comes out with a few moist crumbs attached. Set the pan on a wire rack to cool for at least 1 hour. Cut the cake into twelve 3-inch × 3¼-inch pieces.

4. Line a 9 × 5-inch loaf pan with wax paper. Place 4 brownies on the bottom of the pan, breaking them as necessary to fit; press them lightly into one layer. Spread the softened coffee ice cream over the brownies. Then place 4 more brownies on top, again breaking them as necessary and pressing them lightly to form a layer. Spread the softened chocolate ice cream over that layer, and repeat with the remaining brownies to make a top to the cake. Cover the loaf pan tightly with plastic wrap and freeze for at least 2 hours, preferably setting the pan on the bottom of the freezer.

5. After unwrapping the cake, unmold it onto a platter. Peel away the wax paper, and slice into ¾-inch-thick servings. To store leftovers, rewrap any uncut cake immediately in plastic wrap and refreeze at once—melting ice cream will turn the cake soggy.

To vary this recipe
Substitute any of the following for one of the ice creams:

banana ice cream • butterscotch ice cream • cherry vanilla ice cream • chocolate fudge ice cream • chocolate sorbet • coconut ice cream • coconut sorbet • mango sorbet • peach ice cream • raspberry sorbet • strawberry ice cream • strawberry sorbet • vanilla ice cream

and/or

Stir ½ cup of any of the following into the batter with the coffee:

chopped pecans • chopped unsalted peanuts • chopped walnuts • cocoa nibs • dried cherries • dried cranberries • Reese's Pieces • white chocolate chips

and/or

Substitute ¼ cup of any of the following for the coffee:

Baileys Original Irish Cream • Frangelico or other hazelnut-flavored liqueur • heavy cream • Kahlúa or other coffee-flavored liqueur • milk (whole or low-fat, but not fat-free).

and/or

This recipe can also be made with any of the cakey brownies in this book such as Banana Brownies (page 14) • Lunchbox Brownies (page 68) • or Malt Brownies (page 70).

Brownie Mix Kahlúa Bars

Makes twenty-four $2\frac{1}{4} \times 2\frac{1}{8}$-inch brownies

Nothing could be easier than this quick way to gussy up a brownie mix. For an easy sauce, simply pour more Kahlúa or other coffee-flavored liqueur over the top of the brownies when you serve them. For even more extravagance, top the brownies with vanilla ice cream and warmed hot fudge sauce.

Unsalted butter for the pan
All-purpose flour for the pan
One 19.9-ounce package brownie mix, or any
  brownie mix suitable for a 9 × 13-inch baking pan
2 large eggs, at room temperature, lightly beaten
8 tablespoons (1 stick) unsalted butter, melted,
¼ cup Kahlúa or other coffee-flavored liqueur

1. Position the rack in the lower third of the oven. Preheat the oven to 350°F. Butter and flour a 9 × 13-inch baking pan; set it aside.

2. Place the brownie mix, beaten eggs, melted butter, and Kahlúa in a large bowl; stir with a wooden spoon until smooth. Pour the batter into the prepared pan, spreading it gently to the corners.

3. Bake for 30 minutes, or until a toothpick or cake tester comes out with a few moist crumbs attached. Set the pan on a wire rack to cool for at least 30 minutes.

4. Cut the brownies into 24 pieces while they're still in the pan. Carefully remove them with an offset spatula. Serve immediately, or let cool completely before covering with plastic wrap for storage at room temperature. They will stay fresh for up to 4 days. The brownies can also be tightly wrapped in wax paper, sealed in a freezer-safe bag, and frozen for up to 3 months; allow them to thaw at room temperature before serving.

To vary this recipe

Substitute ¼ cup of any of the following for the Kahlúa:

Baileys Original Irish Cream • bourbon • Chambord or other raspberry-flavored liqueur • Cherry Heering • Frangelico or other hazelnut-flavored liqueur • gold rum • Limoncello or other lemon-flavored liqueur • Pernod or other anise-flavored liqueur • whiskey

and/or

Stir in 1 cup of any of the following with the liqueur:

chocolate-covered espresso beans • chopped banana chips • chopped dried figs • chopped dried pineapple • chopped pecans • chopped walnuts • dried cranberries • dried currants • milk chocolate chips • raisins • Reese's Pieces • semisweet chocolate chips • white chocolate chips.

Brownie Mix Lemon Bars

Makes twenty-four 2¼ × 2⅛-inch brownies

Classic tart, creamy lemon bars are reinvented with this quick, made-from-a-mix brownie crust. For fancier treats, top each bar with chocolate sprinkles, colored sugar, or even candied violets.

Unsalted butter for the pan

FOR THE CRUST

One 19.9-ounce package brownie mix, or any
   brownie mix suitable for a 9 × 13-inch baking pan
1 large egg, at room temperature, lightly beaten
6 tablespoons (1 stick) unsalted butter, melted

FOR THE FILLING

4 large eggs, at room temperature
2 cups sugar
2 tablespoons all-purpose flour
½ cup lemon juice

FOR THE TOPPING

Confectioners' sugar

1. Position the rack in the lower third of the oven. Preheat the oven to 350°F. Butter a 9 × 13-inch baking pan; set it aside.

2. Place the brownie mix, beaten egg, and melted butter in a large bowl; stir with a wooden spoon until well combined—the dough will be quite thick. Press into the prepared pan, covering the bottom and extending up the sides about ½ inch.

3. Bake for 10 minutes. Set the pan on a wire rack to cool while you prepare the filling. Maintain the oven temperature.

4. To make the filling, whisk the eggs until frothy and light in a large bowl, about 2 minutes. Add the sugar, flour, and lemon juice; continue whisking until the sugar has dissolved and the mixture is smooth and pale yellow, about 3 minutes. Pour the filling over the warm crust, and bake for 20 minutes, or until the filling begins to brown and is set when the pan is shaken.

5. Set the pan on a wire rack to cool completely, about 2 hours. Dust the lemon bars with confectioners' sugar; then cut into 24 pieces while still in the pan. Carefully remove them with an offset spatula. They will stay fresh for up to 3 days, covered tightly with plastic wrap.

To vary this recipe
Substitute ½ cup of any of the following for the lemon juice:
lime juice • orange juice • tangerine juice
and/or
Mix ½ cup of any of the following into the brownie crust with the melted butter:
chopped pecans • chopped toasted hazelnuts • chopped walnuts • cocoa nibs • shredded sweetened coconut.

Brownie Mix Marzipan Sandwich Squares

Makes sixteen 2¼ × 2¼-inch brownies

For this easy, almondy brownie recipe, use only fresh, soft marzipan or almond paste. If it's even slightly hard, the marzipan will crumble and break when you roll it out. These small chocolate sandwiches can be iced with any thick frosting, such as Brown Sugar Icing (page 148) or Chocolate Fudge Frosting (page 152).

Unsalted butter for the pan
All-purpose flour for the pan
One 7-ounce tube marzipan or almond paste
One 19.9-ounce package brownie mix, or any brownie mix suitable for a 9 × 13-inch baking pan
3 large eggs, at room temperature, lightly beaten
8 tablespoons (1 stick) unsalted butter, melted
¼ cup milk (whole, low-fat, or fat-free)

1. Position the rack in the lower third of the oven. Preheat the oven to 350°F. Butter and flour a 9-inch square baking pan; set it aside.

2. Sprinkle the work surface with a few drops of water, then lay a 10-inch sheet of wax paper on top. (The water will keep it from slipping.) Flatten the marzipan slightly against the wax paper with your palm, then top with a second sheet of wax paper. Roll the marzipan into an 8-inch square using a heavy rolling pin.

3. Place the brownie mix, beaten eggs, melted butter, and milk in a large bowl; stir with a wooden spoon until smooth. Pour half the batter into the prepared pan, spreading it gently to the corners. Top with the square of marzipan; then spoon the remaining batter over the top, again spreading it gently to the corners.

4. Bake for 45 minutes, or until a toothpick or cake tester comes out clean. Set the pan on a wire rack to cool for at least 30 minutes.

5. Cut the brownies into 16 pieces while they're still in the pan. Carefully remove them with an offset spatula. Serve immediately, or let cool completely before covering with plastic wrap for storage at room temperature. They will stay fresh for up to 4 days. The brownies can also be tightly wrapped in wax paper, sealed in a freezer-safe bag, and frozen for up to 3 months; allow them to thaw at room temperature before serving.

To vary this recipe
Substitute any of the following for the milk:
Amaretto or other almond-flavored liqueur •
Chambord or other raspberry-flavored liqueur

• Cointreau or other orange-flavored liqueur • Frangelico or other hazelnut-flavored liqueur • Kahlúa or other coffee-flavored liqueur

and/or

Add ¾ cup of any of the following to the batter with the eggs:

chopped pecans • chopped unsalted peanuts • chopped walnuts • cocoa nibs • dried blueberries • dried cherries • dried cranberries • raisins • raspberry chocolate chips • shredded unsweetened coconut • white chocolate chips.

Brownie Mix Muffins

Makes 12 muffins

Although these chocolate muffins are great for breakfast, they're good any time of the day, even as a dessert with ice cream or vanilla pudding. You can take this doctored brownie-mix recipe to even more decadent heights by following some of the variations ideas, given below.

12 paper muffin cups
2 large eggs, at room temperature
1 large egg yolk, at room temperature
One 19.9-ounce package brownie mix, or any brownie mix suitable for a 9 × 13-inch baking pan
8 tablespoons (1 stick) unsalted butter, melted
¼ cup milk (whole, low-fat, or fat-free)

1. Position the rack in the lower third of the oven. Preheat the oven to 350°F. Line a 12-muffin tin or two 6-muffin tins with paper muffin cups; set aside.

2. Lightly beat the eggs and egg yolk in a large bowl. Add the brownie mix, melted butter, and milk; stir with a wooden spoon until smooth. Place a scant ⅓ cup batter into each lined muffin cup.

3. Bake for 25 minutes, or until a toothpick or cake tester comes out clean. Set the muffin tins on a wire rack to cool for 10 minutes. Unmold the muffins and serve immediately or allow to cool to room temperature on a wire rack. They will stay fresh for up to 4 days, covered tightly at room temperature. They can also be wrapped tightly in plastic wrap, then sealed in a freezer-safe bag, and frozen for up to 2 months; allow them to thaw at room temperature before serving.

To vary this recipe
Stir ¾ cup of any of the following into the batter with the milk:
butterscotch chips • chopped pecans • chopped toasted hazelnuts • chopped walnuts • peanut butter chips • semisweet chocolate chips • sliced almonds • toasted pepitás • toasted pinenuts • white chocolate chips
and/or
Press one of any of the following into the middle of each of the brownie muffin before baking (you'll need a total of 12 pieces):
1-inch caramels • 1-inch peanut butter cups • 1-inch pieces of nougat • mini Almond Joy bars • mini Mounds bars • Riesen • Rolos • small chocolate truffles.

Brownie Mix Peach Cobbler

Makes 8 servings

A cobbler is a simple dish, "cobbled" together at the last minute; this technique makes it even easier. The crumbled brownie topping becomes crunchy but also melts into the filling, giving the peaches a deep chocolaty flavor. Serve the cobbler in bowls, along with cherry vanilla or peach ice cream.

Unsalted butter for the pan

FOR THE FILLING
One 2-pound package frozen peach slices, thawed; or 6 fresh peaches, peeled, pitted, and sliced
½ cup sugar
3 tablespoons quick-cooking tapioca
½ teaspoon ground cinnamon
½ teaspoon salt
¼ teaspoon grated nutmeg

FOR THE TOPPING
2 large eggs, at room temperature
1 large egg yolk, at room temperature
One 19.9-ounce package brownie mix, or any brownie mix suitable for a 9 × 13-inch baking pan
6 tablespoons unsalted butter, melted

1. Position the rack in the lower third of the oven. Preheat the oven to 350°F. Butter a 9 × 13-inch baking pan; set it aside.

2. To make the fruit filling, place the peach slices in a large bowl. Toss with the sugar, tapioca, cinnamon, salt, and nutmeg; set aside for 10 minutes to macerate.

3. Meanwhile, make the topping: Lightly beat the eggs and egg yolk in a large bowl until frothy. Add the brownie mix and melted butter; stir with a wooden spoon until well combined. The mixture will be quite thick.

4. To make the cobbler, spoon the fruit mixture into the prepared pan, evenly distributing it throughout; then spoon the brownie batter over it, covering as much of the top as possible.

5. Bake for 55 minutes, or until the fruit filling is bubbling and a toothpick or cake tester comes out of the brownie topping with a few moist crumbs attached. Set the pan on a wire rack to cool for at least 15 minutes; then serve immediately. The cobbler will stay fresh for up to 2 days, tightly covered at room temperature.

To vary this recipe
Substitute equivalent amounts of any of these frozen fruits for the frozen peach slices: blueberries • mixed fruits • raspberries • strawberries

or

Substitute 6 cups fresh apple slices for the frozen peaches

and/or

Stir ⅔ cup of any of the following into the brownie topping with the melted butter: chopped pecans • chopped toasted hazelnuts • chopped toasted pepitás • chopped walnuts • cocoa nibs • shredded unsweetened coconut.

Brownie Mix Peanut Butter Cup Squares

Makes sixteen 2¼ × 2¼-inch brownies

These decadent treats are so simple that you can have a crowd-pleaser ready in no time at all. The peanut butter cups melt into the batter, making it moist and even richer. To go all out, ice these brownies with Buttercream (page 150) or Seven Minute Frosting (page 164).

Unsalted butter for the pan
All-purpose flour for the pan
One 19.9-ounce package brownie mix, or any
  brownie mix suitable for a 9 × 13-inch baking pan
3 large eggs, at room temperature, lightly beaten
8 tablespoons (1 stick) unsalted butter, melted,
  plus additional butter for greasing the pan
¼ cup milk (whole, low-fat, or fat-free)
16 miniature peanut butter cups, such as Reese's
  Miniatures, paper wrappers removed

1. Position the rack in the lower third of the oven. Preheat the oven to 350°F. Butter and flour a 9-inch square baking pan; set it aside.

2. Place the brownie mix, beaten eggs, melted butter, and milk in a large bowl; stir with a wooden spoon until smooth. Spoon the batter into the prepared pan, spreading it gently to the corners. Press the miniature peanut butter cups into the batter in a grid so that each will become the center of a cut brownie—that is, in a 4 × 4 grid. Push the cups in so that their tops are even with the top of the batter.

3. Bake for 35 minutes, or until a toothpick or cake tester—inserted near the center but where there's no peanut butter cup—comes out with a few moist crumbs attached. Set the pan on a wire rack to cool for at least 30 minutes.

4. Cut the brownies into 16 squares while they're still in the pan, making sure each piece has a peanut butter cup in it. Carefully remove the brownies with an offset spatula. Serve immediately, or let cool completely before covering with plastic wrap for storage at room temperature. They will stay fresh for up to 4 days. The brownies can also be tightly wrapped in wax paper, sealed in a freezer-safe bag, and frozen for up to 3 months; allow them to thaw at room temperature before serving.

To vary this recipe
Substitute ¼ cup of any of the following for the milk:
apple cider • Cointreau or other orange-flavored liqueur • Frangelico or other hazelnut-flavored liqueur • Kahlúa or other coffee-flavored liqueur • unsweetened coconut milk
and/or
Stir 2 teaspoons of ground cinnamon • or ground ginger into the batter with the milk
and/or
Stir ½ cup chopped pecans • or chopped walnuts into the batter with the milk

Brownie Mix Pie

Makes 8 servings

This chocolaty pie has the flavor and consistency of those creamy fudge pies popular in restaurants and bakeshops across the country. Serve slices topped with sweetened whipped cream, or with a dollop of Lemon Curd (page 159) on the side.

1 ready-to-bake 10-inch frozen pie crust, defrosted; or 1 homemade pie shell, unbaked
1 cup peanut butter chips
One 19.9-ounce package brownie mix, or any brownie mix suitable for a 9 × 13-inch baking pan
2 large eggs, at room temperature, lightly beaten
10 tablespoons (1 stick plus 2 tablespoons) unsalted butter, melted

1. Position the rack in the lower third of the oven. Preheat the oven to 350°F. Line a 10-inch pie plate with the pie crust. Sprinkle the peanut butter chips over the crust.

2. Place the brownie mix, beaten eggs, and melted butter in a large bowl; stir with a wooden spoon until smooth. Drop table-spoonsful of the thick batter into the pie shell, covering it completely. Spread the batter gently to cover any holes, but try not to push the chips to the sides.

3. Bake for 30 minutes, or until the filling is set; then place on a wire rack to cool. Cool completely before cutting. The pie will stay fresh for up to 4 days, covered tightly in the refrigerator; bring to room temperature before serving.

To vary this recipe
Substitute butterscotch chips • mint chocolate chips • or white chocolate chips for the peanut butter chips
and/or
Stir ½ cup of any of the following into the brownie batter with the melted butter:
chopped banana chips • chopped pecans • chopped walnuts • dried cranberries • raisins
and/or
Stir any one of the following flavorings into the brownie batter with the melted butter:
2 teaspoons vanilla extract • 2 teaspoons ground cinnamon • 2 teaspoons ground ginger • 1 teaspoon almond extract.

Brownie Mix Pineapple-Upside-Down Cake

Makes 8 servings

This easy cake is best made in a cast-iron skillet—one that can get so hot that the sugar will caramelize between the pineapple slices. When you turn the cake upside down on a platter, the deep, dark syrup runs down the sides, like a sauce. Arrange the pineapple slices attractively in the pan, since they become the cake's "decoration" when it's inverted. Serve with sweetened whipped cream or homemade mango sorbet.

14 tablespoons (1¾ sticks) unsalted butter, at room temperature
1 cup packed dark brown sugar
One 20-ounce can pineapple rings in juice or heavy syrup, drained, ¼ cup of the juice reserved
One 19.9-ounce package brownie mix, or any brownie mix suitable for a 9 × 13-inch baking pan
3 large egg yolks, at room temperature, lightly beaten
4 large egg whites, at room temperature, beaten until soft peaks form

1. Position the rack in the lower third of the oven. Preheat the oven to 350°F.

2. Melt 8 tablespoons (1 stick) butter in a heavy cast-iron skillet set over medium heat; stir in the brown sugar and cook, stirring constantly, until the sugar melts and the mixture bubbles.

Continue cooking for 2 minutes, stirring constantly.

3. Blot the pineapple rings dry; then place them on the bottom of the skillet, overlapping as necessary. Set aside.

4. Melt the remaining 6 tablespoons (¾ stick) butter in a separate small pan over low heat, or in the microwave on High for 40 seconds. Place the melted butter, brownie mix, reserved juice, and beaten egg yolks in a large bowl; stir until thick and smooth.

5. Beat half the whipped egg whites into the brownie batter, using a mixer at medium speed. Then gently fold the remaining egg whites into the batter, using a rubber spatula. There may be white streaks in the batter. Pour the batter over the pineapple rings, spreading it gently to the edges of the skillet.

6. Place the skillet on a large lipped cookie sheet, and bake for 50 minutes. A toothpick or cake tester will come out with a few moist crumbs attached. Set the skillet on a wire rack to cool for at least 30 minutes, then unmold the cake onto a round lipped cake plate. The cake will stay fresh for up to 4 days, covered tightly at room temperature.

To vary this recipe

Substitute canned peaches • or canned pears for the pineapple rings (slice the peaches and pears into thin strips)

and/or

Stir ½ cup of any of the following into the brownie batter with the beaten egg yolks: chopped pecans • chopped toasted hazelnuts • chopped walnuts • semisweet chocolate chips • or white chocolate chips.

Brownie Mix Rocky Road Bars

Makes twenty-four 2¼ × 2⅛-inch brownie bars

Rocky Road candy was popularized in the 1920s, at a time when the roads across the nation were first being paved; the bumps of marshmallows and nuts looked, of course, like old country roads. Since a rocky road was a primitive one, this candy was popularized as a "homemade" Ozark delight. (It was actually a Fannie Farmer recipe picked up by a nut company.) Here we've brought that classic combination of marshmallows, nuts, and chocolate to a doctored brownie mix for a quick and easy treat.

Unsalted butter for the pan
All-purpose flour for the pan
One 19.9-ounce package brownie mix, or any brownie mix suitable for a 9 × 13-inch baking pan
3 large eggs, at room temperature, lightly beaten
8 tablespoons (1 stick) unsalted butter, melted
¼ cup milk (whole, low-fat, or fat-free)
3 cups mini marshmallows
1 cup chopped walnuts
6 ounces semisweet chocolate chips (about 1 cup), or chopped semisweet chocolate

1. Position the rack in the lower third of the oven. Preheat the oven to 350°F. Butter and flour a 9 × 13-inch baking pan; set it aside.

2. Place the brownie mix, beaten eggs, melted butter, and milk in a large bowl; stir with a wooden spoon until smooth, then pour into the prepared pan. Bake for 30 minutes, or until a toothpick or cake tester comes out with a few moist crumbs attached.

3. The moment the pan is out of the oven and on a wire rack, sprinkle the marshmallows over the top, followed by the nuts and the chocolate chips. Cover the pan with aluminum foil to hold in the heat for 5 minutes; then uncover the pan and cool for an additional 30 minutes.

4. Cut the brownies into 24 pieces while they're still in the pan. Carefully remove them with an offset spatula. Serve immediately, or let cool completely before covering tightly with plastic wrap for storage at room temperature for up to 4 days. The brownies can also be tightly wrapped in wax paper, sealed in a freezer-safe bag, and frozen for up to 3 months; allow them to thaw at room temperature before serving.

To vary this recipe
Substitute chopped pecans for the walnuts
and/or
Substitute butterscotch chips • milk chocolate chips • mint chocolate chips • peanut butter

chips • or white chocolate chips for the semi-sweet chocolate chips

and/or

Stir any of the following flavorings into the batter with the milk:

1 tablespoon vanilla extract • 2 teaspoons rum extract • 2 teaspoons ground cinnamon • 1 teaspoon almond extract.

Brownie Mix S'mores

Makes twenty-four 2¼ × 2⅛-inch brownie s'mores

Don't wait for your next camp-out or picnic to try this summertime favorite of chocolate, marshmallows, and graham crackers. S'mores are even easier with a brownie mix—and ready for your next outing any time of the year.

Unsalted butter for the pan
All-purpose flour for the pan
One 19.9-ounce package brownie mix, or any
  brownie mix suitable for a 9 × 13-inch baking pan
3 large eggs, at room temperature, lightly beaten
8 tablespoons (1 stick) unsalted butter, melted
¼ cup milk (whole, low-fat, or fat-free)
2 cups mini marshmallows
Ten to twelve whole graham crackers (2½ × 5
  inches)

1. Position the rack in the lower third of the oven. Preheat the oven to 350°F. Butter and flour a 9 × 13-inch baking pan; set it aside.

2. Place the brownie mix, beaten eggs, melted butter, and milk in a large bowl; stir with a wooden spoon until smooth, then pour into the prepared pan. Bake for 25 minutes or until a toothpick or cake tester comes out with a few moist crumbs attached. Place the pan on a wire rack. Maintain the oven temperature.

3. The moment the pan is out of the oven, sprinkle the mini marshmallows over the top; then cover with the graham crackers, breaking some as necessary to cover the entire pan. Place the pan back in the oven and bake for 2 minutes to melt the marshmallows. Remove the pan and gently press the graham crackers down into the melted topping. Be careful—it will be very hot.

4. Cool the pan completely on a wire rack; then turn it over to unmold the cake onto a cutting board. Place a wire rack over the cake and invert once again, so that the graham crackers are back on top. Cut the s'mores into 24 pieces. They will stay fresh for up to 2 days, covered tightly at room temperature.

To vary this recipe
Stir 1 cup of any of the following into the batter with the milk:
chopped banana chips • chopped dried figs • chopped dried pineapple • chopped pecans • chopped walnuts • cocoa nibs • dried cranberries • dried currants • milk chocolate chips • peanut butter chips • raisins • Reese's Pieces • semisweet chocolate chips • shredded unsweetened coconut • white chocolate chips.

Brownie Mix Soufflé Cake

Makes 8 servings

As with any soufflé, the egg whites cause this fudgy cake to rise up high in the hot oven, then fall slightly as it cools. Springform pans are available at cooking stores and some gourmet stores, or from outlets listed in the Source Guide. This cake is best served warm.

Unsalted butter for the pan
All-purpose flour for the pan
One 19.9-ounce package brownie mix, or any brownie mix suitable for a 9 × 13-inch baking pan
3 large egg yolks, at room temperature, lightly beaten
8 tablespoons (1 stick) unsalted butter, melted
¼ cup milk (regular or low-fat, but not fat-free)
4 large egg whites, at room temperature, beaten until soft peaks form

1. Position the rack in the lower third of the oven. Preheat the oven to 400°F. Butter and flour a 9-inch springform pan; set it aside.

2. Place the brownie mix, beaten egg yolks, melted butter, and milk in a large bowl; stir with a wooden spoon until smooth. Beat in half the whipped egg whites with a wire whisk until the batter is uniform and thick; then gently fold in the remaining beaten egg whites with a rubber spatula. There may be white streaks in the batter. Pour it into the prepared pan.

3. Place the pan on a lipped baking sheet to catch any drips, and bake for 30 minutes. The cake is done when the middle is set when the pan is shaken. Set the pan on a wire rack to cool for 10 minutes; the cake will fall immediately.

4. Unfasten the sides of the pan and transfer the cake to a cake plate or other serving tray. Serve immediately, with sweetened whipped cream or ice cream. The cake will stay fresh for up to 4 days, tightly covered at room temperature.

To vary this recipe
Substitute ¼ cup of any of the following for the milk:
Baileys Original Irish Cream • bourbon • Chambord or other raspberry-flavored liqueur • Cherry Heering • Frangelico or other hazelnut-flavored liqueur • gold rum • Kahlúa or other coffee-flavored liqueur • Limoncello or other lemon-flavored liqueur • Pernod or other anise-flavored liqueur • whiskey.

Brownie Mix Strudel

Makes two 10 × 4-inch strudels

Believe it or not, a brownie mix makes a quick and easy filling for a classic strudel. Phyllo dough, which traditionally makes this dessert's light flaky crust, has an unjustified reputation for being hard to work with. If you let the box thaw unopened overnight on a lipped tray or cookie sheet in the refrigerator, then keep the dough covered on your work surface with a towel moistened with only a few drops of water, the paper-thin sheets are actually quite easy to use. If one tears, simply patch the hole with a small piece from another phyllo sheet.

Vegetable oil spray or unsalted butter for the pan
One 19.9-ounce package brownie mix, or any
   brownie mix suitable for a 9 × 13-inch baking pan
2 large eggs, at room temperature, lightly beaten
¼ cup vegetable oil
2 tablespoons heavy cream
1 cup finely chopped walnuts
¼ cup sugar
1 teaspoon ground cinnamon
One 1-pound package phyllo dough, thawed
Vegetable oil spray, or 8 tablespoons unsalted
   butter, melted, for moistening the phyllo dough

1. Position the rack in the lower third of the oven. Preheat the oven to 350°F. Lightly spray a large baking sheet with vegetable oil or grease it with butter; set it aside.

2. Place the brownie mix, beaten eggs, vegetable oil, and cream in a large bowl; stir with a wooden spoon until smooth, then set aside. In a second bowl, combine the walnuts, sugar, and cinnamon; set aside.

3. Unfold the phyllo dough and cover it with a towel moistened with 6 or 7 drops of water. Place one phyllo sheet on the work surface; lightly spray it with vegetable oil or brush it with melted butter. Place a second sheet on top of the first, and again lightly spray with vegetable oil or brush with melted butter. Repeat with a third sheet, then sprinkle with ¼ cup walnut mixture. Cover with a fourth phyllo sheet. Lightly spray or brush with melted butter, then sprinkle another ¼ cup walnut mixture over the top. Top with a fifth sheet of dough, and lightly spray or brush with melted butter. Spoon half the brownie batter down the middle of the length of the dough—drop the batter by heaping tablespoonsful so you don't have to spread it and possibly break the phyllo sheets. Leave at least 1 inch of pastry clear at each end of the dough. Fold these ends loosely over the dough; then roll the strudel up along its length. Roll it very loosely, leaving room for the brownie dough to rise as it bakes. The strudel should be about 4 inches wide.

4. Place the strudel seam-side-down on the prepared baking sheet. Spray the top lightly with vegetable oil or brush it with melted butter; sprinkle 2 tablespoons of the walnut mixture over the top.

5. Repeat the process with the remaining dough, brownie filling, and walnut mixture for a second strudel. Reserve any unused phyllo for another use. Place the second strudel on the same baking sheet as the first.

6. Bake the strudels for 35 minutes, or until golden brown. Set the baking sheet on a wire rack to cool for at least 20 minutes; then remove the strudels from the sheet and allow them to cool on the wire rack. Serve immediately, or cover tightly with plastic wrap for storage at room temperature. They will stay fresh for up to 2 days.

To vary this recipe
Substitute chopped pecans • chopped pistachios • chopped toasted hazelnuts • sliced almonds • or toasted pinenuts for the walnuts.

Brownie Mix Tiramisù

Makes 12 servings

Tiramisù (literally "pick me up" in Italian) is a coffee-flavored cream-and-cake pastry, popular as a midafternoon snack in Italy. Most of us, however, know it as an American dessert craze, popularized in the 1980s. This version, with a brownie-mix crust, takes no time at all and will soon become a standard in your repertoire of easy, elegant favorites. It's even better the second day, after the flavors have a chance to meld.

FOR THE CAKE

Unsalted butter for the pan
All-purpose flour for the pan
One 19.9-ounce package brownie mix, or any
  brownie mix suitable for a 9 × 13-inch baking pan
3 large eggs, at room temperature, lightly beaten
8 tablespoons (1 stick) unsalted butter, melted
¼ cup milk (regular, low-fat, or fat-free)

FOR THE CREAM FILLING AND TOPPING

2 cups ricotta cheese (regular, low-fat, or fat-free)
2 tablespoons instant espresso powder dissolved
  in ½ cup hot water
2 tablespoons granulated sugar
2 cups heavy cream
2 tablespoons confectioners' sugar
1 tablespoon vanilla extract
½ cup brandy
2 tablespoons unsweetened cocoa powder

1. Position the rack in the lower third of the oven. Preheat the oven to 350°F. Butter and flour a 9 × 13-inch baking pan; set it aside.

2. Place the brownie mix, beaten eggs, melted butter, and milk in a large bowl; stir with a wooden spoon until smooth, then pour into the prepared pan. Bake for 30 minutes or until a toothpick or cake tester comes out clean. Cool the pan on a wire rack for 30 minutes. Cut the brownies into twelve 3-inch squares. Carefully remove them with an offset spatula, and allow them to cool completely on the rack. The brownies can be made up to 2 days ahead; cover tightly in plastic wrap and keep at room temperature.

3. To make the filling: In a medium bowl, whisk the ricotta cheese, espresso mixture, and sugar until smooth and well combined. Set aside.

4. In a large bowl, whip the cream until bubbly with an electric mixer at high speed; add the confectioners' sugar and vanilla, and continue beating until soft peaks form, about 2 minutes. Set aside.

5. Place half the brownies in the bottom of a 10-inch round or 10-cup oval baking dish;

break them up as necessary to fit. Sprinkle the brownies with ¼ cup brandy; then spread half the cheese mixture over the top. Cover with half the whipped cream. Repeat with another layer of brownies, brandy, cheese mixture, and whipped cream. Sift the cocoa powder over the top. Cover tightly and refrigerate until ready to serve. The tiramisù will keep fresh for up to 3 days, covered in the refrigerator.

To vary this recipe
Use Lunchbox Brownies (page 68) • or Cake Brownies (page 34).

Substitute bourbon • gold rum • Kahlúa or other coffee-flavored liqueur • Southern Comfort • or whiskey for the brandy
and/or
Stir ⅔ cup chopped pecans or chopped walnuts into the batter with the milk
and/or
Substitute 1½ teaspoons almond extract for the vanilla extract in the whipped cream

Brownie Mix Truffle Squares

Makes sixteen 2¼ × 2¼-inch squares

Chocolate truffles are dark, rich candies that take their name from the rare, dark, and delicious Périgordian root fungus so highly prized by gourmands worldwide. Purchased chocolate truffles melt into these easy brownies, creating a chewy, rich center. If you want, ice these brownies with Marshmallow Cream Frosting (page 160)—or Ganache Icing (page 157) for a chocolate lover's fantasy.

Unsalted butter for the pan
All-purpose flour for the pan
One 19.9-ounce package brownie mix, or any brownie mix suitable for a 9 × 13-inch baking pan
3 large eggs, at room temperature, lightly beaten
8 tablespoons (1 stick) unsalted butter, melted
¼ cup milk (regular, low-fat, or fat-free)
Sixteen 1-inch-diameter purchased chocolate truffles

1. Position the rack in the lower third of the oven. Preheat the oven to 350°F. Butter and flour a 9-inch square baking pan; set it aside.

2. Place the brownie mix, beaten eggs, melted butter, and milk in a large bowl; stir with a wooden spoon until smooth, then spread into the prepared pan. Gently press the truffles into the batter in a grid so that each will become the center of a cut brownie—that is, in a 4 × 4 grid.

Push them down so that their tops are even with the top of the batter.

3. Bake for 35 minutes or until a toothpick or cake tester—inserted near the center of the pan but not in a truffle—comes out with a few moist crumbs attached. Set the pan on a wire rack to cool for at least 1 hour.

4. Cut the brownies into 16 squares while they're still in the pan, making sure each square has a truffle in the middle. Carefully remove them with an offset spatula. Serve immediately, or let cool completely before covering tightly with plastic wrap for storage at room temperature. They will stay fresh for up to 4 days. The brownies can also be tightly wrapped in wax paper, sealed in a freezer-safe bag, and frozen for up to 3 months; allow them to thaw at room temperature before serving.

To vary this recipe
Substitute ¼ cup of any of the following for the milk:
Baileys Original Irish Cream • bourbon • Chambord or other raspberry-flavored liqueur • Cherry Heering • Cointreau or other orange-flavored liqueur • Frangelico or other hazelnut-flavored liqueur • gold rum • Kahlúa or other coffee-flavored liqueur • Pernod or other anise-flavored liqueur • whiskey.

Brownie Mix Turtle Bars

Makes twenty-four 2¼ × 2⅛-inch brownie bars

Turtle candies—pecans covered in caramel and chocolate—have long been a holiday treat, made popular by several national candy companies and by the Neiman Marcus Christmas catalog. This recipe doctors a mix so that the brownies become much like that candy treat—but you can easily enjoy these all year long.

Unsalted butter for the pan
All-purpose flour for the pan
One 19.9-ounce package brownie mix, or any
  brownie mix suitable for a 9 × 13-inch baking pan
3 large eggs, at room temperature, lightly beaten
  until frothy
8 tablespoons (1 stick) unsalted butter, melted
¼ cup plus 2 tablespoons evaporated milk
  (regular or low-fat, but not fat-free)
1 cup chopped pecans
½ cup caramels, such as Kraft
3 ounces semisweet chocolate chips
  (about ½ cup)

1. Position the rack in the lower third of the oven. Preheat the oven to 350°F. Butter and flour a 9 × 13-inch baking pan; set it aside.

2. Place the brownie mix, beaten eggs, melted butter, ¼ cup evaporated milk, and pecans in a large bowl; stir with a wooden spoon until smooth. Pour two-thirds of this batter into the prepared pan, spreading it gently to the corners. Bake for 8 minutes.

3. Meanwhile, melt the caramels and the remaining 2 tablespoons evaporated milk in a small saucepan set over medium-low heat; stir constantly until the mixture is smooth. When the brownie cake has baked for 8 minutes, remove the pan from the oven, set it on a wire rack, and sprinkle the chocolate chips over the top. Drizzle the melted caramel mixture over the cake. Dot the remaining brownie batter over the top to cover it. Do not spread the batter, or the melted caramels will be pushed to the side.

4. Bake for 20 minutes, or until the brownies begin to pull away from the sides of the pan. Set the pan on a wire rack to cool completely.

5. Cut the brownies into 24 pieces while they're still in the pan. Carefully remove them with an offset spatula. Serve immediately, or cover with plastic wrap for storage at room temperature. They will stay fresh for up to 4 days. The brownies can also be tightly wrapped in wax paper, sealed in a freezer-safe bag, and frozen for up to 2 months; allow them to thaw at room temperature before serving.

To vary this recipe

Substitute chopped walnuts for the pecans
and/or
Mix any of the following flavorings into the brownie batter with the pecans:

1 tablespoon vanilla extract • 2 teaspoons rum extract • 2 teaspoons ground cinnamon • 1 teaspoon almond extract.

Source Guide

Appliances.com
www.w.appliances.com
888-543-8345
11558 State Route 44
Mantua, OH 44255
Great prices on mixers and other baking appliances.

Boyajian
www.boyajianinc.com
800-419-4677
349 Lenox Street
Norwood, MA 02062
Although some flavors are available at gourmet markets, the entire collection of extracts is available on Boyajian's website.

Bridge Kitchenware
www.bridgekitchenware.com
212-688-4220
214 E. 52nd Street
New York, NY 10022
A complete selection of baking supplies including mixers, pans, and bowls.

BulkCandyStore.com
www.bulkcandystore.com
561-615-8646
Extremely low prices on candies and dried fruits.

Central Market
www.centralmarket.com
800-360-2552
4001 North Lamar
Austin, TX 78756
Possibly the best gourmet supermarket in the United States. Many varieties of chocolates, nuts, dried fruits, and flavorings are available.

Kitchen Krafts
www.kitchenkrafts.com
800-776-0575
Many specialty baking tools, chocolate choppers, and flavorings.

Marshall's Farm Honey
www.MarshallsHoney.com
800-624-4637
155-159 Lombard Road
American Canyon, CA 94503
Some of the best honey available, by phone, at
the farm store, at Bay Area farmer's markets,
and at a few California retailers.

New York Cake and Baking Distributors
800-942-2539 or 212-675-CAKE
56 West 22nd Street
New York, NY 10010
A full range of flavorings, along with all kinds of
chocolate, cocoa nibs, and baking pans.

Orange Tree Imports
www.orangetreeimports.com
608-255-8211
1721 Monroe Street
Madison, WI 53711
Mixers and other baking supplies—online, on
the phone, or in person.

Penzeys Spices
www.penzeys.com
800-741-7787
Incredibly fresh spices in bulk, as well as
arrowroot and double-strength vanilla.

Scharffen Berger Chocolate Maker, Inc.
www.scharffenberger.com

800-930-4528
914 Heinz Avenue
Berkeley, CA 94710
Handmade chocolate from the finest blend of
cocoa beans, as well as the best source of cocoa
nibs. Although some of their products are
available in many gourmet stores, everything
can be bought directly on their website.

Williams-Sonoma
www.williams-sonoma.com
800-541-2233
P.O. Box 7456
San Francisco, CA 94120
Mixers, bowls, baking pans, and many
flavorings, available online or at one of their
many nationwide stores.

Zabars
www.zabars.com
800-697-6301 or 212-496-1234
2245 Broadway
New York, NY 10024
Mixers, baking pans, bowls and other kitchen
supplies, as well as chocolate, flavorings, nuts,
and dried fruits.

"Ultimate" Cookbooks
www.ultimatecook.com
Recipes and information on all the
"Ultimate" books as well as restaurant tips,
travel ideas, and an idea for a cooking party
with friends.

Index

cola:
    brownies, 50–51
    icing, 154
cookies:
    brownie, 22–23
    brownie mix, 172
cornbread brownies, 52–53
corn oil, 8
cranberry brownies,
    54–55
cream cheese:
    blondies, 124–25
    brownies, 56–57
    frosting, 155

Double boilers, 9

Eggs, 6, 9
equipment, 6–7
    baking pans, 3, 4, 8–9, 10,
      11
    cake testers, 5, 10
    chocolate choppers, 4
    double boilers, 9
    fine-meshed sieves, 10
    flour sifters, 10
    kitchen scales, 4
    knives, 11
    microwave ovens, 9–10
    mixers, 4–5
    offset spatulas, 5
    rubber spatulas, 10, 11
    sieves, 10
extract:
    banana, 7
    maple, 7
    mint, 7
    peppermint, 7, 86
    rum, 7
    vanilla, 6, 7–8

Fat-free brownies, 58–59
five minute chocolate frosting,
    156
flavorings, 3, 7–8
flour:
    all-purpose, 7
    arrowroot, 62
    unbleached, 7
    whole wheat, 146–47
flour sifters, 10
frostings, 148–66
    chocolate fudge, 152
    cocoa, 153
    cream cheese, 155
    five minute chocolate,
      156
    grasshopper, 158
    marshmallow cream,
      160
    mocha cream, 162
    seven minute, 2, 12, 164
    see also icings
fruitcake blondies, 126–27
fudge:
    brownies, 60–61
    frosting, chocolate, 152

Ganache icing, 157
gingerbread blondies,
    128–29
gluten-free brownies,
    62–63
grasshopper frosting, 158

mixers, 4–5
mocha cream frosting, 162
muffins, brownie mix, 180

Nut oils, 8
nuts, 8
    toasting of, 10

Oat:
    blondies, 142–43
    brownies, 88–89
offset spatulas, 5

Pancakes, brownie, 24–25
Passover brownies, 90–91
peach cobbler, brownie mix,
    181–82
peanut butter:
    blondies, 144–45
    brownies, 92–93
    cup squares, brownie mix, 183
    icing, 163
pear brownies, 94–95
pepitás, 8
peppermint extract, 7, 86
pie, brownie mix, 184
pineapple-upside-down cake, brownie mix,
    185–86
pumpkin brownies, 96–97

Rocky road bars, brownie mix,
    187–88
rum extract, 7

Seven minute frosting, 164
sieves, fine-meshed, 10
s'mores, brownie mix,
    189
soufflé cake, brownie mix,
    190
sour cream:
    brownies, 98–99
    icing, 165
soy lecithin, 6
spatulas:
    offset, 5
    rubber, 10, 11
spices, 3
squares:
    crunch, Heath bar brownie mix,
        173
    marzipan sandwich brownie mix,
        178–79
    peanut butter cup, brownie mix,
        183
    truffle, brownie mix, 195
strudel, brownie mix, 191–92
sugar, 6
sweet corn brownies, 100–101
sweet potato brownies, 102–3

Tiramisù, brownie mix,
    193–94
truffle squares, brownie mix,
    195
turtle bars, brownie mix,
    196–97

Vanilla extract, 6, 7–8
    double-strength, 8
    icing, 166

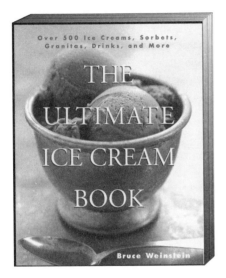
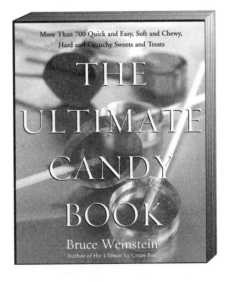

THE ULTIMATE PARTY DRINK BOOK
*Over 750 Recipes for Cocktails,
Smoothies, Blender Drinks,
Nonalcoholic Drinks, and More*

ISBN 0-688-17764-6 (paperback)

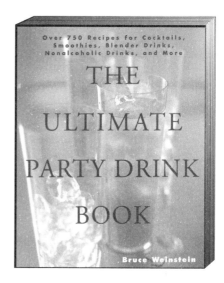

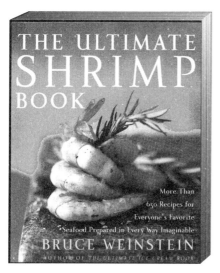

THE ULTIMATE SHRIMP BOOK
*More Than 650 Recipes for Everyone's
Favorite Seafood Prepared in Every
Way Imaginable*

ISBN 0-06-093416-6 (paperback)

THE ULTIMATE POTATO BOOK
*Hundreds of Ways to Turn America's
Side Dish into a Meal*

By Bruce Weinstein and Mark Scarbrough

ISBN 0-06-009675-6 (paperback)